Accounting comparisons

UK and IASC

Accounting comparisons

UK and IASC

Compiled by Christopher Nobes
Coopers & Lybrand Professor of Accounting
University of Reading

London, November 1996

Also in this series:

Accounting Comparisons: UK, Netherlands, France and Germany

This book aims to provide general guidance only and does not purport to deal with all possible questions and issues that may arise in any given situation. Should the reader encounter particular problems he is advised to seek professional advice, which Coopers & Lybrand would be pleased to provide.

No responsibility for loss occasioned to any person acting or refraining from action as a result of any material in this publication can be accepted by the author.

Coopers & Lybrand is authorised by the Institute of Chartered Accountants in England and Wales to carry on investment business.

ISBN 1 85355 752 8

© Coopers & Lybrand, November 1996

All rights reserved. No part of this publication may be reproduced, stored in any retrieval system, or transmitted in any form or by any means, electronic, mechanical, photocopying, recording, or otherwise, without the prior permission of the publisher.

Preface

This book is designed for those who are familiar with UK accounting. Consequently, the book concentrates on explanations of IASC rules. UK rules are brought in for comparison purposes, and there is a detailed treatment of *differences* between UK and IASC rules. Readers are asked to look at the 'Introduction' for more detail on this.

I am grateful to Peter Holgate and Helen McCann of the Accounting Technical Department of Coopers & Lybrand (London) for suggestions for improvement. Nevertheless, these colleagues are not responsible for errors or omissions. Further, although I am a representative on the Board of the IASC, this should not be taken to mean that the IASC necessarily agrees with the opinions contained herein.

This book was completed in October 1996, after the approval of a revision to IAS 12. The pace of change is such that readers should be alert for changes since then which may affect the comparisons made here.

Christopher Nobes

Contents

Introduction	1
UK and IASC rule making	3
UK regulatory framework	3
IASC standard setting	4
IASC's relationships	7
Relevance of IASC	7
Conceptual frameworks and future developments	8
A note on the appendices	9
IASC and UK rules for asset valuation	11
Property, plant and equipment	11
Investment properties	13
Investments	14
Research and development	17
Government grants	19
Leases	21
Stocks/inventories	26
Construction contracts	29
Assets and liabilities in a foreign currency	30
Financial instruments	32
IASC and UK rules for profit measurement	35
Depreciation	35
Taxation	39
Extraordinary items etc	44
Revenue recognition	46
Pensions	48
IASC and UK rules for group accounting	53
Consolidation of subsidiaries	53
Associates	56
Joint ventures	57
Acquisitions and mergers	59
Goodwill and fair values	62
Currency translation of financial statements	65

IASC and UK rules in other areas 69
  Policies, disclosures, formats 69
  Cash flow statements 71
  Contingencies and post balance sheet events 74
  Segmental reporting 75
  Changing prices 77
  Related party disclosures 78

IASC's work in progress 81

Summary and concluding remarks 85
  Compatibility of UK and IASC rules until 1993 85
  Compatibility after 1993 85
  Implications of the incompatibilities 89

UK and IASC rules 93

Equivalence between UK and IASC rules 97

Introduction

This book concentrates on International Accounting Standards (IASs) and on the *differences* between them and UK rules. The viewpoint taken is that of an accountant familiar with UK rules and practice. That is, topics covered by IASs but not in the UK are dealt with here in the same detail as topics covered by both sets of rules. However, topics dealt with by the UK but *not* by IASs are merely listed in Table 1.1 on page 10. 'UK rules' here means SSAPs, FRSs, UITF abstracts and the Companies Act 1985 (as amended). It does not include the rules of the London Stock Exchange. Further details on UK rules can be found in the Coopers & Lybrand *Manual of Accounting*.

The differences recorded in this book are, of course, only those which appear to be significant. However, the exact wordings of UK and IASC documents on a particular topic are nearly always different. So, even when the intention appears to be identical, there is an uncountably large number of potential differences in interpretation. Particularly in the case of required disclosures, various minor differences have been omitted here. Interpretation of IASs is addressed by *Understanding IAS: Analysis and interpretation* published by Coopers & Lybrand.

Topic headings in chapters 2 to 5 generally relate to particular accounting standards of the UK or the IASC, whichever are narrower. For example, the UK's SSAP 9 deals with inventories and long-term contracts, which are covered by IAS 2 and IAS 11 respectively. Therefore, two headings are used here.

This book concerns the financial reporting of general industrial and commercial companies. There are many special UK rules for banks, insurance companies, pensions funds, charities, etc which are not dealt with here. In some cases, there are also IASC rules in these areas: for example, IAS 26 covers similar ground to the UK's SORP on pension fund accounting; and IAS 30 concerns disclosures by banks and other financial institutions.

Chapter 1

UK and IASC rule making

UK regulatory framework

1.1 UK accounting rules exist within a legal framework. Since the Companies Act 1947, British companies have been required by law to publish audited annual accounts containing a large number of disclosures. The accounts are required to give a true and fair view. However, before the 1981 Act (now consolidated into the 1985 Act), most detailed rules of accounting measurement, valuation and presentation were not to be found in law but in accounting standards or 'generally accepted practice'. Many rules can now be found in the Companies Act 1985, as amended by the Companies Act 1989. Much of the contents of the Companies Acts in the 1980s derived from the need to implement the second, fourth, seventh and eighth Directives on company law of the European Communities.

1.2 Accounting standards resulted from the setting up, in late 1969, of the Accounting Standards Committee[1] (ASC), which was controlled by the UK and Irish professional accountancy bodies. This committee issued Statements of Standard Accounting Practice (SSAPs) until July 1990. SSAPs had no legal authority, although legal opinion suggested that they would be influential in the determination by a Court as to whether a set of annual accounts gave a true and fair view. Auditors were required to qualify their reports if a true and fair view was not given, which might be the case if SSAPs had been departed from.

1.3 In 1990, the ASC was closed down and replaced by an independent body, the Accounting Standards Board (ASB). Coinciding with this, the Companies Act 1989 recognised the new standard setting machinery and required directors of public and other large companies to disclose whether or not standards have been complied with. The ASB adopted all existing SSAPs and began to issue its own Financial Reporting Standards (FRSs).

---

[1] Originally called the Accounting Standards Steering Committee, set up by the Institute of Chartered Accountants in England and Wales.

1.4 As part of the new machinery, a Review Panel was established. The Panel is empowered under the law to take directors to Court for issuing accounts which fail to comply with the law, for example, fail to give a true and fair view. Various penalties are set out. The publicity attached to an investigation by the Review Panel and the threat of legal action have persuaded companies to comply with the Review Panel's recommendations.

1.5 A further part of the machinery is the Urgent Issues Task Force (UITF), a subsidiary of the ASB. This body attempts to achieve a consensus on interpretations of existing rules in controversial areas. The resulting 'abstracts' are intended to be followed in order to enable a true and fair view to be given.

1.6 Legal counsel's opinion suggests that the status of standards has been greatly strengthened by the changes of 1989/90, and that, *prima facie*, standards and UITF abstracts have to be followed in order to give a true and fair view.

IASC standard setting

1.7 In Sydney in 1972, a world congress of accountants was held, at which discussions leading to the IASC's formation were conducted. Sir Henry (later Lord) Benson played a leading role in this and he became IASC's first chairman. The IASC began work in 1973. Its aims are (Preface, 1983):

- to formulate and publish in the public interest accounting standards to be observed in the presentation of financial statements and to promote their worldwide acceptance and observance, and

- to work generally for the improvement and harmonisation of regulations, accounting standards and procedures relating to the presentation of financial statements.

1.8 The members of the IASC are professional bodies throughout the world (more than 110 of them from more than 85 countries). They promise to 'use their best endeavours' to persuade national standard setters to publish statements in accord with International Accounting Standards (IASs) and to work for acceptance of IASs by companies, auditors and exchange regulators.

1.9 The IASC is independent from other bodies, but from 1983 a close relationship with the International Federation of Accountants (IFAC) was forged, whereby the two bodies work together but in different fields. For example, IFAC deals with auditing standards. The member bodies of IFAC and IASC are identical and part of the funding of IASC comes through IFAC. The founder members of IASC were professional accountancy bodies from:

- Australia
- Canada
- France
- Germany (Federal Republic)
- Japan
- Mexico
- The Netherlands
- UK and Ireland
- USA

1.10 In 1996, all of these are Board members. The remaining seven current Board members are:

- India (with Sri Lanka)
- Malaysia
- Nordic Federation of Public Accountants
- South Africa (with Zimbabwe)
- Federation of Swiss Industrial Holding Companies
- International Co-ordinating Committee of Financial Analysts' Associations
- International Association of Financial Executives Institutes

1.11 The Board generally meets for about one week three or four times per year. A two-thirds majority of the Board is necessary to issue an exposure draft and a three-quarters majority for a standard.

1.12 In order to make progress, the Board often had to retain some widely used options in its standards so that sufficient Board votes could be obtained and so that companies in many countries could follow IASs without too great a difficulty.

1.13 In order to advance the IASC's work, it was decided in the late 1980s to begin a programme of reviewing major standards in order to improve them, particularly by removing as many options as possible, so that IASs constituted a tighter set of standards. This was called the comparability or improvements project. One objective was to persuade securities regulators, particularly IOSCO[2] and its US member the SEC, to accept financial statements drawn up in accordance with IASs for multinational listings. Such statements are already accepted on several exchanges (for example, London) but not on others (for example, New York).

1.14 The IASC published its comparability exposure draft (E 32) in 1989. This led to the release of many exposure drafts and standards in the subsequent years. The process was completed at the end of 1993 with the issue of ten revised standards, which came into force in 1995.

1.15 A new feature of the revised standards (and of recent exposure drafts) is that any remaining options are specifically pointed out and divided between 'benchmark treatments' and 'allowed alternatives'. Companies must disclose their accounting policies, although in most cases numerical reconciliation to the benchmark is not required. An exception to this is that those adopting the LIFO allowed alternative for inventory valuation under IAS 2 must disclose the numerical effect of this. The IASC does not mean to imply that the benchmark treatment is the preferred one. The terms are really only labels for the two alternatives.

1.16 IOSCO's response to the IASC's revisions of 1993 was to note the improvements and to suggest a list of further changes that would be necessary in order to accept the IASs as 'core standards' for use by companies with cross-border listings. In 1995, IASC and IOSCO announced a detailed four-year programme towards achieving this aim. IASC has since ambitiously suggested that it may be possible to complete the programme in the first half of 1998.

1.17 A further development of 1996 was IASC's decision to establish a Standing Interpretations Committee which would serve a somewhat similar function to the UK's UITF.

---

[2] International Organisation of Securities Commissions.

IASC's relationships

1.18 The relationship with IOSCO has been noted above. In 1996, IOSCO began to send representatives as observers to the IASC Board. Other observers include representatives from the European Commission and the US Financial Accounting Standards Board.

1.19 There are also occasional meetings of IASC's Consultative Group, which includes a wide range of interested bodies, such as the World Bank.

Relevance of IASC

1.20 Up to the end of 1993, a UK company which complied with UK rules would generally have been in conformity with IASC standards in all material respects. However, this is not the case for the revised IASC standards of 1993 onwards, as the following chapters of this book show. Further inconsistencies are likely to emerge over the next few years, as explained in the next section of this chapter. This means that UK companies who wish to present accounts in conformity with IASs (perhaps for some overseas purpose) will now have to put some effort into discovering the UK/IASC differences and into adjusting their accounting practices.

1.21 Several other areas where the IASC's work is relevant and which may affect UK companies, auditors or analysts are:

- *Large companies in the developed world.* In several countries, some large listed corporations are using IASs in whole or in part for group annual reports. Usually, this is for foreign capital raising. At present this is noticeable for Canada, Finland, France, Germany, Italy, Sweden and Switzerland. As IASs become tighter and diverge from UK rules (for example), large UK companies seeking foreign listings may need to know about IASs.

- *Developing countries.* Given that many developing countries adopt IASs (or amend them slightly), there are several countries with very rapid growth rates where knowledge of IASs is central to preparation, audit and interpretation of accounts or to advice to companies.

- *Emerging countries.* Governmental bodies, other standard-setters and stock exchanges will be seeking guidance on the development of national standards. The respectability and international nature of the IASC suggest that advice on the basis of IASs may be accepted. For newly emerging large companies in these countries, the same point applies.

- *Investors, lenders, fund managers, brokers, analysts.* Investors and lenders, whether individual or corporate, will increasingly find that annual reports from around the world are prepared wholly or partly using IASs. Advice will be needed on how to interpret and compare this with other rules.

- *Accountancy firms.* As the world continues to become more international, the need to train staff in different rules, including IASs, will increase in order to serve the above parties. Firms that are too small or too insular to keep up with this process may need help and may be uncompetitive.

- *Tax authorities, labour unions, other interested parties.* There are many other users of financial statements who have to operate in the globalising market. They will meet IASs with increasing frequency and may need assistance.

- *Transnational authorities.* Bodies such as the EC Commission, IOSCO, the UN, the OECD, The World Bank, the IMF and the EBRD will increasingly meet IASs and may need orientation or recommendations.

Conceptual frameworks and future developments

1.22 The IASC published its 'Framework for the Preparation and Presentation of Financial Statements' in 1989. This bears a fairly close relationship to the conceptual framework developed in the USA by the FASB from the middle 1970s. In the late 1980s the UK's ASC acknowledged the IASC's framework and began to make use of it from time to time. Also, definitions of 'asset' and 'liability' found their way into exposure drafts of the late 1980s on accounting for the substance of transactions. The ASB published draft chapters of its own statement of principles in the first few years of its life. The contents are also closely in line with IASC's framework.

1.23 Several important developments in IASC rules can be predicted from existing projects. These are examined in Chapter 6.

A note on the appendices

1.24 There are two appendices to this book. Appendix 1 shows a list of UK and IASC standards. Appendix 2 gives tables of equivalence from UK documents to IASC documents and *vice versa*. Table 1.1 in this chapter lists those topics covered by UK rules but not by IASC rules. These issues are not dealt with in detail elsewhere in this book. By contrast, areas dealt with by the IASC but not by UK rules *are* covered in detail in later chapters. As mentioned earlier, this approach is taken on the assumption that most readers are starting from a basis of knowledge of UK rules and wishing to understand IASC rules.

Table 1.1 Topics covered by UK rules but not by the IASC

1. *Value Added Tax.* SSAP 5 requires accounting figures to be shown net of VAT. There is no equivalent IAS.

2. *The Treatment of Taxation under the Imputation System.* SSAP 8 deals with the treatment of ACT and tax credits in the financial statements. There is no equivalent IAS.

3. *Presentation of Profit and Loss Accounts, including Provisions.* FRS 3 imposes a layered presentation. There is no equivalent IAS, although an Exposure Draft (E 53) on the presentation of financial statements was published in 1996. FRS 3 also has detailed requirements relating to the timing and disclosure of provisions on the sale of businesses. These have no equivalents in IASC rules, although IASC steering committees were working on 'discontinuing operations' and on 'provisions' from 1996.

4. *Substance of Transactions.* FRS 5 sets out a detailed approach to accounting for the substance of transactions in cases not directly covered by other rules. Although IAS 1 requires the use of substance over form, there are no detailed IASC instructions on this. IAS 1 will be revised as part of the 'presentation' project discussed above.

5. *Earnings per Share.* The expression 'earnings per share' is defined by SSAP 3 (as amended in 1992) and listed companies are required to disclose this in the profit and loss account. There is no equivalent IAS, although an Exposure Draft (E 52) on this was issued by the IASC in 1996. The UK's ASB also issued this for discussion, with a view to minimising differences between UK and IASC rules.

Chapter 2

IASC and UK rules for asset valuation

2.1 This chapter looks at IASC rules and at differences between them and UK rules in the area of the valuation of assets. Some related issues (such as depreciation) are covered in Chapter 3, which deals with profit measurement rules.

Property, plant and equipment

2.2 The IASC's rules on this subject are to be found in IAS 16 (revised 1993). The main requirements are as follows:

- Property, plant and equipment (PPE) should be recognised when (a) it is probable that future benefits will flow from it and (b) its cost can be measured reliably (paragraph 8).

- Initial measurement should be at cost (paragraph 15).

- Subsequently, the benchmark treatment is to use cost but the allowed alternative is to use an up-to-date fair value by class of assets (paragraphs 29, 30 and 36).

- Revaluations should be credited to reserves unless reversing a previous charge to income. Decreases in valuation should be charged to income unless reversing a previous credit to reserves (paragraphs 39 and 40).

- If an asset's recoverable amount falls below its carrying amount, the decline should be recognised and charged to income (unless it reverses a previous credit to reserves) (paragraph 56).

- Gains or losses on retirement or disposal of an asset should be calculated by reference to the carrying amount (paragraph 62).

- Disclosures should include a reconciliation of the carrying amount of each class of PPE from the beginning to the end of the period (paragraph 66).

Differences between UK and IASC rules

2.3 The following box summarises the main *differences* between UK and IASC rules which are then dealt with in more detail.

UK	IASC
Source	
CA 1985	IAS 16
Valuation	
Wide choice of valuation methods (Sch 4, paras 17 and 31).	Benchmark: historical cost (para 29). Alternative: re-value classes of assets at fair value (on a regular basis so as to avoid material differences from fair value) (paras 30 and 36).
Diminutions in value	
Permanent diminutions in value should be charged to income except to the extent that they are covered by revaluation reserves related to the same asset. (Sch 4, para 19). There is no requirement to recognise temporary diminutions in value.	When recoverable amount falls below carrying amount or when a downward revaluation occurs, write downs should be charged to income unless covered by revaluation reserves related to the asset (paras 40 and 56). No distinction is made between temporary and permanent diminutions.

Valuation

2.4 The flexible UK rules on valuations would allow any practices acceptable under IAS 16. However, the reverse is not the case. If there is departure from historical cost under IAS 16, then revaluation must be done by class of asset and at fair value at the balance sheet date. A class of assets is a grouping of assets of a similar nature, such as machinery (paragraph 37). This all means that the common UK approach of occasional revaluation of selected assets is not acceptable under IAS 16.

Diminutions in value

2.5 There is no clear general requirement for an impairment test on items of fixed assets in the UK. By contrast, IAS 16 (paragraph 56) requires a periodic review of individual assets (or groups of identical assets) to check whether recoverable amount has fallen below carrying amount. Recoverable amount is the expected recovery from future use, including residual value (paragraph 7). The IASC was preparing an exposure draft on 'impairments' in 1996.

Investment properties

2.6 IAS 25 (reformatted 1994) covers accounting for investments, including investment properties which are defined as those that are not occupied substantially for use by the reporting enterprise or in its group (paragraph 4). The IAS allows investment properties either to be treated as other property, plant and equipment under IAS 16 or as investments under IAS 25. These two IASs are covered in the preceding and following sections of this book.

Differences between UK and IASC rules

2.7 The box below summarises the *differences* between UK and IASC rules. Where one source of rules provides no instruction, a '–' is shown below.

UK	IASC
Source	
SSAP 19	IAS 25
Treatment	
Requires annual revaluation to open market value and no depreciation (paras 9 and 10).	Permits periodic revaluation and therefore no depreciation (para 28). Otherwise see Investments on page 14.
Disclosures	
Particulars of valuers (para 12).	–
–	Fair values of properties if they are accounted for as investments (para 49).

2.8 In summary, the UK rules of SSAP 19 are more specific than those under IASs. By following certain options in IAS 25, it would be possible to be consistent with the requirements of SSAP 19. However, as noted in Section 2.1, the treatment of revaluation deficits may differ.

Investments

2.9 Accounting for investments is covered by IAS 25 (reformatted 1994), the main requirements of which are:

- Current investments are those readily realisable and intended to be held for up to one year (paragraph 4).

- Investment properties should either be treated as normal property (see IAS 16) or as long-term investments (paragraph 28).

- Current investments should be valued at market or at the lower of cost and market, for which a portfolio basis is acceptable (paragraph 19).

- Long-term investments should be valued at cost, or revaluation by category, or (for marketable equity securities) at the lower of cost or market on a portfolio basis. Permanent diminutions in value should be recognised and measured on an individual basis (paragraph 23).

- Where current investments are carried at market value, increases or decreases in value can either be consistently taken to income or treated as revaluation surpluses or deficits. In the latter case, a decrease should be charged to income unless it offsets a previous surplus on the same investment (paragraphs 31 and 32).

- For long-term investments reclassified as current investments, the transfer value depends upon how the long-term investments were valued (paragraph 36). Investments reclassified from current to long-term should be transferred at the lower of cost and market, or at market if they were previously stated at that value (paragraph 37).

2.10 IAS 25 is likely to be revised soon, particularly when new rules on financial instruments are agreed.

Differences between UK and IASC rules

2.11 The box below relates to the *differences* between IASC and UK rules, although most of these relate to options or to matters for which there are no specific rules in one case or the other. Some of these points are then discussed in more detail.

UK	IASC
\multicolumn{2}{c}{*Source*}	
CA 1985; FRS 3; UITF 5	IAS 25; IAS 27; IAS 28
Current asset definition	
Not intended for continuing use in the business (s 262(1)).	Readily realisable and intended to be held for up to one year (IAS 25, para 4).
Current asset valuation	
Value at lower of cost and net realisable value or at current cost (Sch 4, paras 22, 23 and 31).	Value at market or at lower of cost and market (IAS 25, para 19).
Fixed asset valuation	
Value at cost or revaluation or other appropriate basis (Sch 4, paras 17 and 31). Provisions for temporary loss of value may be made (Sch 4, para 19).	Value at cost or revalued amounts, or (for marketable securities) at lower of cost and market, determined on a portfolio basis (IAS 25, para 23).
Gains and losses	
For current assets held at market value, ('marking to market'), it is not clear whether gains or losses can be taken to income without resort to a 'true and fair' override (Sch 4, para 31).	For current assets held at market value, gains or losses can be included in income, or can be credited to a revaluation surplus (IAS 25, para 31).
Disposals of revalued investments	
The gain or loss reported in income must be calculated by reference to the carrying amount (FRS 3, para 21). Any revaluation surplus should be transferred to retained earnings.	On disposal, the revaluation surplus can either be taken to income or transferred to retained earnings (IAS 25, para 33).
Subsidiaries or associates in parent accounts	
Accounted for as fixed asset investments.	May be accounted for using the equity method or at cost or revalued amounts (IAS 27, para 29; and IAS 28, para 12).

	Fixed to current asset transfers
–	In cases where current investments are carried at lower of cost and market, transfer at the lower of cost and carrying amount. Reverse any revaluation reserve. Where current investments are carried at market, transfer carrying amount. Transfer any remaining revaluation reserve to income if the policy on current assets is to take gains and losses to income (IAS 25, para 36).
	Current to fixed asset transfers
Transfer at the lower of cost and net realisable value at date of transfer. Charge any loss to income (UITF 5).	Transfer at lower of cost and market or at market (if that was the basis used) (IAS 25, para 37).
	Disclosure
Market value of listed investments, if this differs from the carrying amount (Sch 4, para 45).	Market value of marketable investments, if not held on this basis (IAS 25, para 49).
Information concerning holdings of 20 per cent or more in another undertaking (other than a subsidiary) (Sch 5, para 7).	–
Must be split between current and fixed (Sch 4, formats).	Should be split between current and fixed, if the balance sheet is classified in this way (IAS 13 allows but does not require such classification) (IAS 25, para 8).
Amounts of investments in listed securities.	–

Gains and losses

2.12 IAS 25 allows the use of marking to market for current assets. Such a practice is followed by some financial institutions in the UK, but creates legal problems for other companies, so it is unusual for them.

Disposals

2.13 An option under IAS 25 is to take revaluation surplus to income on disposal of a revalued asset. This is not now allowed in the UK. The IAS optional practice would obviously give higher income.

Research and development

2.14 IAS 9 (revised 1993) contains the requirements for accounting for research and development costs. The following are the main provisions:

- IAS 9 does not apply to costs of exploration and development of oil, gas and mineral deposits (paragraph 3). There are presently no IASC rules in these areas.

- Research and development are separately defined. Development is the application of research to production (paragraph 6).

- R&D costs include those directly attributable on a reasonable basis (paragraph 11).

- Research costs should be expensed when incurred (paragraph 15).

- Development costs should be expensed unless they meet certain criteria (paragraph 16).

- Development costs meeting all the following criteria must be capitalised (paragraph 17):
    - clearly defined product or process;
    - costs separately identified and reliably measured;
    - technical feasibility demonstrable;
    - enterprise intends to proceed;
    - usefulness demonstrable; and
    - adequate resources demonstrable.

- Capitalised costs should not exceed probable net recovery (paragraph 17).

- Amortisation should be systematic and reflect related benefits (paragraph 21).

- Capitalised costs should be written down if net recovery becomes improbable or if the criteria cease to be met (paragraph 23).

- Write downs should be reversed, allowing for the amortisation that would have been charged, if there is persuasive evidence of the continuing reversal of the circumstances that led to write down (paragraph 27).

- There should be reconciliation of the change in the unamortised balance of development costs (paragraph 30).

2.15 IASC decided in 1996 to revise IAS 9 in order to eliminate any inconsistencies with the requirements for other intangible assets. An exposure draft is expected in 1997.

Differences between UK and IASC rules

2.16 Both UK and IASC rules prohibit the capitalisation of research expenses and have similar criteria to be satisfied for the capitalisation of development expenses. Disclosure requirements are also largely similar. The box below deals with the *differences*, some of which are discussed below.

UK	IASC
Source	
SSAP 13; CA 1985	IAS 9
Deferral	
An option when conditions are met (SSAP 13, para 25), but should be adopted consistently (SSAP 13, para 27).	Required when conditions are met (para 17).
Re-instatement	
–	Development costs, if initially expensed, cannot later be capitalised (para 16).
–	If the reasons for impairment of an asset reverse, the amount written down should be reinstated (para 27).

	Disclosure
R&D expense for the period, except that private companies below certain size limits have an exemption (SSAP 13, para 22).	R&D expense for the period (para 30).
Reasons for capitalising (Sch 4, para 20(2)).	–

Deferral

2.17 The criteria to allow (SSAP 13) or require (IAS 9) deferral are very similar. IAS 9, unlike SSAP 13, requires the enterprise to 'intend to produce and market, or use, the product or process' (paragraph 17). However, it seems unlikely that this would lead to differences in practice.

Re-instatement

2.18 IAS 9's requirement that expensed costs cannot subsequently be capitalised even if they meet the criteria seems not to be consistent with the Framework. However, it is probably an anti-avoidance provision.

Amortisation

2.19 The commencement date for amortisation under IAS 9 (paragraph 22) is when the product or process is *available* for sale or use. Under SSAP 13 (paragraph 28) the date relates to commercial production or application. In practice, this will probably not lead to differences because IAS 9 requires amortisation with respect to actual sale or use.

Government grants

2.20 IAS 20 (reformatted 1994) regulates the accounting treatment of government grants. Its main requirements are:

- Government grants should not be recognised until there is reasonable assurance that they will be received and that the conditions attached to them will be complied with (paragraph 7).

- Grants should be recognised as income in a way which matches the costs to be compensated (paragraph 12).

- Where there are no future related costs, grants should be recognised when receivable (paragraph 20).

- Grants related to assets should be deducted from cost or treated as deferred income (paragraph 24).

- Repayment of a grant should be treated as a revision to an estimate (paragraph 32).

Differences between UK and IASC rules

2.21 There are many similarities between SSAP 4 and IAS 20, but there are some differences:

UK	IASC
Source	
SSAP 4	IAS 20
Treatment	
Deferred amounts of grants should be treated as deferred income. For undertakings not subject to Sch 4 of the Companies Act, grants can be deducted from the cost of the fixed asset (para 25).	Deferred amounts of grants should be treated as deferred income or deducted from the asset (para 24).
–	A forgivable loan from government is treated as a grant when there is reasonable assurance that the terms for forgiveness will be met (para 10).
Repayment of grant	
Potential liabilities to repay should only be accrued if repayment is probable (para 27).	Cumulative additional depreciation that would have been charged in the absence of the grant should be charged immediately (para 32).
Disclosures	
The effects of the grants on results and financial position. Nature and effects of governmental non-grant assistance (para 28).	Nature and extent of grants recognised. Indication of other government assistance. Unfulfilled conditions etc on recognised grants (para 39).

Treatment

2.22 IAS 20 and SSAP 4 offer the same choice of treatment for grants related to assets. However, SSAP 4 has to recognise that, for some enterprises, there is a British legal problem, with the deduction method.

2.23 Although SSAP 4 does not cover forgivable loans, IAS 20's requirement seems consistent with SSAP 4.

Repayment

2.24 IAS 20 contains more detail than SSAP 4 about how to charge a repayment. However, it seems likely that the same result would follow under both standards.

Leases

2.25 IAS 17 (reformatted 1994) regulates accounting for leases. The main requirements are:

- Finance leases are those which transfer substantially all risks and rewards to the lessee (paragraph 3).

- Finance leases should be capitalised at the lower of the fair value and the present value of the minimum lease payments (paragraph 11).

- Rental payments should be split into (i) a reduction of the liability and (ii) a finance charge designed to reduce in line with the liability (paragraph 14).

- Depreciation on leased assets should be calculated using useful life, unless there is no reasonable certainty of eventual ownership. In the latter case, the shorter of useful life and lease term should be used (paragraph 16).

- Operating leases should be expensed on a systematic basis (paragraph 19).

- For lessors, finance leases should be recorded as receivables (paragraph 28).

- Lease income should be recognised on the basis of a constant periodic rate of return (paragraph 30).

- Manufacturer or dealer lessors should include selling profit on the same basis as that for sales (paragraph 39).

- Lessors should recognise rental income on operating leases on a straight line basis or on a basis more representative of the pattern of earnings (paragraph 46).

- For a sale and leaseback resulting in a finance lease, any excess of proceeds over carrying amount should be deferred and amortised over the lease term (paragraph 57).

- For sale and leaseback resulting in an operating lease, profit or loss should be recognised immediately, unless the sale price is not fair value (paragraph 59).

- For operating leases where fair value at the time of sale and leaseback is less than carrying amount, a loss should be recognised immediately (paragraph 61).

Differences between UK and IASC rules

2.26 Although the broad approaches of UK and IASC rules in this area are similar, there are many differences of detail, upon which this book concentrates in the box below. The topic is divided into four sections: (i) lessee and lessor, (ii) lessee, (iii) lessor and (iv) sale and leaseback. A few of these issues are taken up in more detail after the box.

UK	IASC
	Source
SSAP 21, UITF 12	IAS 17

(i) Lessee and lessor

Definition of finance lease

Lease that transfers substantially all the risks and rewards. This should be assumed if the present value of the minimum lease payments is substantially all (normally 90 per cent or more) of the fair value, using the interest rate implicit in the lease (para 15).	Lease that transfers substantially all the risks and rewards (para 3).

Lease term

Period for which the lessee has contracted to lease the asset and any further terms for which the lessee has the option to continue the lease where it is reasonably certain at the inception of the lease that the option will be exercised (para 19).	The non-cancellable period for which the lessee has contracted to lease the asset together with any further terms, etc (para 3).

(ii) Lessee

Initial capitalisation of a finance lease

At present value of minimum lease payments, although in practice fair value can be used unless it is more than the present value (paras 32-34).	At fair value, or present value of minimum lease payments, if lower (para 11).

Depreciation period

Shorter of useful life and lease term for finance leases. Useful life for hire purchase (para 36).	Useful life, unless no certainty about purchase, when the shorter of useful life and lease term should be used (para 16).

Operating leases

Charge rental on straight line basis unless another method is more appropriate (para 37). Incentives received should be spread over the lease term or, under some circumstances, a shorter period (UITF 12).	Charge rental on a systematic basis representative of time pattern of benefit (para 19).

Disclosure by lessee

Gross amounts of assets and accumulated depreciation and the period's charge by class of asset (para 49). However, net amount of asset can be shown (para 50).	Amounts of assets subject to finance leases (para 21).

Liabilities (and annual operating lease commitments) should be analysed into current, 2-5 years and 5+ years (paras 52 and 56).	Liabilities (including those on non-cancellable operating leases) should be analysed in summary into amounts and periods (para 24).
Aggregate finance charge and operating rentals for the year (paras 53 and 55).	–
–	Significant financing restrictions, options and contingencies (para 26).

(iii) Lessor

Asset in the case of finance lease

Net investment should be reduced for bad or doubtful receivables (para 38).	–

Lessor's income

Total gross earnings should be allocated to give a constant rate of return on the net cash investment, although net investment can usually be used for hire purchase (para 39). Alternatively, an allocation may first be made for cost of finance (para 40).	Allocation on the basis of a constant return on either net investment or net cash investment, used consistently for leases of a similar character (para 30).

Grants for lessor

Tax-free grants should be spread over the lease period (para 41).	–

Manufacturer/dealer

No profit on operating leases. Profit on finance leases restricted to excess of fair value over cost less grants (para 45); and restricted in other ways to allow for marketing effects on pricing (guidance notes, para 148).	If artificially low rates of interest are quoted, selling profit should be restricted (para 39).

IASC and UK rules for asset valuation

Disclosures by lessors	
Net investment in finance leases and HP contracts (para 58).	Gross investment in finance leases and related unearned finance income and unguaranteed residual values (para 51).
Gross amounts of assets held for use in operating leases and related accumulated depreciation (para 59).	Same disclosures as SSAP 21, by class, when significant part of business (para 54).
Aggregate rentals of the period for finance and operating leases; costs of lease assets acquired in the period; policies for leases and, in detail, for finance lease income (para 60).	Basis of allocating income, including whether net investment or net cash investment basis (para 53).
(iv) Sale and leaseback	
Accounting by seller/lessee	
According to SSAP 21, an apparent profit on finance lease to be taken over shorter of lease term and useful life (para 46). However, the guidance notes to SSAP 21 and the provisions of FRS 5 generally mean that profit is not recognised.	Apparent profit on finance lease (if recognised) should be taken over lease term (para 57).
For operating leases: (i) where price is below fair value, a loss compensated by future rentals at below market price should be amortised over lease term, (ii) where price is above fair value, the excess is amortised over the shorter of the lease term and the time to next rent review (para 47).	As for SSAP 21, except that for (i) and (ii) amortisation should be over the period of use (para 59). If the fair value is less than the carrying amount, a loss should be recognised immediately (para 61).

Definition

2.27 The definitions of a finance lease in IAS 17 and SSAP 21 are very similar, but SSAP 21 provides a suggested numerical threshold. This may mean that it is somewhat easier to avoid capitalisation under IAS 17.

2.28 It should be noted that FRS 5 may be relevant here for the UK, in cases where its provisions are more detailed than those of SSAP 21. In particular, this includes lease transactions which form part of a complex arrangement or which contain options, conditional provisions or guarantees. FRS 5 requires emphasis to be placed on those aspects of a transaction that are likely to have commercial effect in practice. This may lead to some leases which appear to be operating leases under SSAP 21 or IAS 17 being treated as finance leases under FRS 5.

2.29 A further problem here is that both the IASC's and the ASB's Framework would suggest that most operating leases meet the definition of assets and liabilities. This may mean that major changes to SSAP 21 and IAS 17 will eventually follow.

Sale and leaseback

2.30 SSAP 21 requires apparent profit on a sale and leaseback to be recognised by deferral and amortisation, but this was restricted by SSAP 21's guidance note 155 and is effectively superseded by FRS 5's application note B. By contrast, IAS 17 merely requires that any profit should not be recognised immediately, allowing the possibility of not recognising it at all.

Stocks/inventories

2.31 Accounting for inventories is covered by IAS 2 (revised 1993). The main requirements are:

- The scope excludes financial instruments and also agricultural products and minerals valued at net realisable value (paragraph 1).

- Inventories should be valued at the lower of cost and net realisable value (paragraph 6).

- Cost includes all costs to bring the inventories to their present condition and location (paragraph 7).

- Where specific cost is not appropriate, the benchmark treatment is to use FIFO or weighted average (paragraph 21).

- An allowed alternative is LIFO, but then there should be disclosure of the lower of (i) net realisable value, and (ii) FIFO, weighted average or current cost (paragraphs 23 and 36).

Differences between UK and IASC rules

2.32 There are many similarities between UK and IASC rules in this area. The points in the box below concern the *differences*, so the common requirements relating to overheads and to disclosures, etc are not covered here.

2.33 Construction contracts are looked at separately as the following topic.

UK	IASC
Source	
SSAP 9; CA 1985	IAS 2
Presentation	
Specific classification required in balance sheet or notes (Sch 4, part I).	Appropriate main categories (para 34).
Cost	
Borrowing costs on amounts financing the production of the asset can be included to the extent that they relate to the period of production (Sch 4, para 26). This is not very common for the production of inventories.	In some circumstances, borrowing costs can be included (para 15).
Costs in non-specific cases	
LIFO can lead to current asset values not related to recent costs. Therefore, it will not normally give a 'true and fair view' (SSAP 9, para 39).	Benchmark: FIFO or weighted average (para 21). Alternative: LIFO (para 23).
Reversal of write downs	
–	When a write down below cost is no longer necessary, the reversal should be recognised as a reduction of the inventory expense (paras 30 and 31).

IASC and UK rules for asset valuation

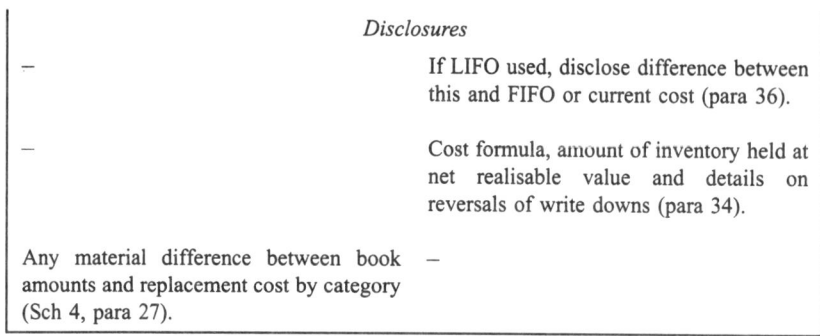

	Disclosures
–	If LIFO used, disclose difference between this and FIFO or current cost (para 36).
–	Cost formula, amount of inventory held at net realisable value and details on reversals of write downs (para 34).
Any material difference between book amounts and replacement cost by category (Sch 4, para 27).	–

Cost

2.34 IAS 2 allows borrowing costs to be capitalised under the conditions of IAS 23, related to inventories requiring a substantial time to mature. By contrast, SSAP 9 (Appendix 1, para 21) suggests that capitalisation will not normally be appropriate for long-term contracts. Therefore, presumably, it is even less appropriate for ordinary inventories. Nevertheless, it may be possible under similar criteria to IAS 23's.

2.35 IAS 2 requires non-interchangeable inventories to be specifically valued whereas others must not be. In principle, SSAP 9 and Sch 4 would allow interchangeable inventories to be specifically valued.

LIFO

2.36 The UK position with respect to LIFO is complex. LIFO is allowed by the Companies Act but not allowed for the calculation of taxable income. SSAP 9 suggests that it will not normally give a true and fair view. This seems to allow that sometimes it will be appropriate, although in practice SSAP 9's comments seem to amount to prohibition.

2.37 By contrast, IAS 2 allows LIFO, although requiring extra disclosures. This is the only case where an IAS requires reconciliation from an allowed alternative to a benchmark treatment.

Construction contracts

2.38   IAS 11 is the source of rules in this area. Its main requirements are:

- A construction contract is one specifically negotiated and relates to an asset or closely related combination of assets (paragraph 3). No particular length of contract is specified.

- Contracts should be treated as separate where there are separate proposals, separate negotiations and separately identifiable costs and revenues (paragraph 8).

- Contract costs include direct costs, those contract costs that can be allocated to the contract and costs chargeable to the customer (paragraph 16).

- When the outcome of a contract can be estimated reliably, revenues and costs should be estimated by stage of completion. Expected losses should be recognised (paragraph 22).

- The conditions for reliable estimation are (paragraph 23):
    - revenue can be reliably measured;
    - it is probable that the benefits will flow to the enterprise;
    - future costs and stage of completion can be measured reliably; and
    - costs can be identified and measured reliably.

- If the outcome cannot be measured reliably, costs should be expensed and revenues should be recognised in line with costs recoverable (paragraph 32).

Differences between UK and IASC rules

2.39   Some differences between UK and IASC rules are noted in the following box:

IASC and UK rules for asset valuation

UK	IASC
	Source
SSAP 9	IAS 11
	Separate or grouped contracts
–	Detailed definitions (paras 7-10).
	Turnover where outcome is uncertain
May show an appropriate proportion of turnover, using a zero estimate of profit (para 10).	Recognise to the extent that costs are probably recoverable (para 32).
	Disclosures
–	Contract revenue in the period (para 39). Aggregate of costs and profits for contracts in progress (para 40).

Separate or grouped contracts

2.40 IAS 11 has some detailed requirements in this area, whereas SSAP 9 merely calls for assessment on a contract by contract basis (paragraph 28). IAS 11 sets out cases where grouping is required. Under the percentage of completion method, the amount and timing of deferral is affected by different groupings.

Assets and liabilities in a foreign currency

2.41 This topic concerns accounting for items in the accounts of an individual entity. The issue of currency translation of foreign entities' financial statements is dealt with from paragraph 4.21.

2.42 The IASC rules are contained in IAS 21 (revised 1993). The main requirements are:

- Foreign currency transactions should be initially recorded using the rate on the transaction date (paragraph 9).

- At each balance sheet date, monetary balances should be reported at the closing rate (paragraph 11).

- Exchange differences which are settled or are due to the use of closing rates should be taken to income unless they relate to a net investment in a foreign entity or a hedge of such (paragraphs 15, 17 and 19).

- An allowed alternative in the case of severe devaluations, is to include differences on a newly acquired asset as part of its carrying amount (paragraph 21).

Differences between UK and IASC rules

2.43 The rules of the UK and the IASC in this area are very similar: basically using closing exchange rates and recognising the resulting gains and losses in income. Both sets of rules allow differences on monetary items that form part of an enterprise's net investment in a foreign entity to be taken to reserves.

2.44 Disclosure requirements are also similar. The points in the box below deal with *differences*.

UK	IASC
Source	
SSAP 20	IAS 21
Forward contracts etc	
If rates of exchange are fixed under the terms of transactions or if there are related or matching forward contracts, the specified rates may be used instead of the year end rates (para 4).	[IAS 21 does not deal with hedge accounting, except for hedges of a net investment, although E 48 did.]
Differences on net investment	
Exchange differences taken to reserves and exchange gains and losses on the borrowing offset against them (para 29).	These differences should be classified as equity until disposal, when they are brought into income (paras 17 and 19).
Severe devaluation	
–	An allowed alternative for such exchange differences (under several conditions) is to include them in the carrying amount of the related asset, subject to review of the carrying amount (para 21).

Forward contracts, etc

2.45 IASC's intention is to deal with hedging in the financial instruments standard. While we wait for this, IASC has announced that IAS 21 does not preclude the deferral of exchange gains and losses on foreign currency hedging instruments.

Financial instruments

2.46 The requirements in this area can be found in IAS 32 (issued in 1995). This standard deals mainly with disclosures, although there are some presentation instructions. Measurement issues were dealt with in exposure drafts E 40 and E 48, but have not yet led to a standard.

2.47 The main requirements of IAS 32 are:

- The IAS does not cover investments in subsidiaries, joint ventures or associates, or pensions and insurance (paragraph 1).

- A financial instrument is a contract giving rise to a financial asset in one enterprise and a financial liability or equity instrument in another (paragraph 5).

- Issuers of financial instruments should classify them according to substance and should split complex instruments into components (paragraphs 18 and 23).

- Interest, dividends, etc should be reported following the above classification (paragraph 30).

- Offsetting of financial assets and liabilities should occur when there is a legally enforceable right of set-off and there is an intention to settle net or simultaneously (paragraph 33).

- For each class of instrument, enterprises should disclose information about its nature and the accounting policies used (paragraph 47); and information about interest rate risk, credit risk and fair value (paragraphs 56, 66 and 77).

- There should be disclosures related to any financial assets held at above fair value or held as hedges (paragraphs 88 and 91).

Differences between UK and IASC rules

2.48 Many of these disclosure requirements are not covered by UK rules. However, the *differences* on the presentation issues are shown in the following box.

UK	IASC
\ *Source*	
FRS 4; FRS 5	IAS 32
Classification as liability/equity	
Classification is generally based on legal form. For example, mandatorily redeemable preference shares should generally be treated as non-equity shares (FRS 4, para 37).	Classification should be based on the substance of an instrument (para 18). For example, mandatorily redeemable preference shares meet the definition of a liability and should be treated as such (para 22). The treatment of dividends, interest, etc should follow the above classification (para 30).
Compound instruments	
Compound instruments should follow their legal form (FRS 4, para 25).	Compound instruments should be separated into component parts of equity and debt (para 23).
Offsetting	
Debit and credit balances should be offset where, and only where, there is ability to insist on net settlement (FRS 5, para 29).	Financial assets and liabilities should be set off when (and only when) there is a legally enforceable right to set off and an intention to use it or to realise the asset and settle the liability simultaneously (para 33).

Classification

2.49 Partly because of legal difficulties, the UK requirements seem to allow form to override substance here, unlike IAS 32's rules. However, where a subsidiary issues shares that meet the definition of a liability for the group, they should be shown as a liability in UK group accounts (FRS 4, paragraph 49).

33

Compound instruments

2.50 IAS 32 requires convertible debentures to be split into equity and liability components, whereas FRS 4 requires them to be treated wholly as liabilities. This also affects the presentation of the income statement, because payments related to the split components are also split into dividends and interest under IAS 32.

Offsetting

2.51 For offsetting, IAS 32 contains the condition that the enterprise intends to settle on a net basis or simultaneously. FRS 5 contains no such criterion, which is consistent with the ASB's attempt to reduce the importance of management intent.

Chapter 3

IASC and UK rules for profit measurement

3.1 This chapter looks at IASC rules and at differences between them and UK rules in the area of profit measurement. Some related issues (such as accounting for construction contracts) are covered in chapter 2, which deals with asset valuation.

Depreciation

3.2 The requirements relating to depreciation of tangible assets are to be found in IAS 16 (revised 1993). IAS 4 is largely superseded by IAS 16, but still applies to intangibles until the IAS on that subject is issued. Diminutions in value, other than systematic depreciation, are covered in Section 2.1. The main requirements of IAS 16 with respect to depreciation are:

- Depreciation should be charged on a systematic basis over useful life, which should be reviewed periodically (paragraphs 43 and 52).

- Changes to useful life and depreciation method are changes in estimates not changes in policy (paragraphs 52 and 55).

Differences between UK and IASC rules

3.3 Although UK and IASC depreciation rules are similar, the latter are considerably less detailed. As usual, this book concentrates on the *differences*, as shown in the box below.

UK	IASC
Source	
SSAP 12	IAS 4; IAS 16
Scope	
Excludes investment properties, goodwill, R&D, investments (para 14).	Excludes forests, mineral exploration, R&D, goodwill (IAS 16, para 1).

	Dismantling, removal, restoration
–	Such costs should be deducted from expected residual value or provided for systematically over useful life (IAS 16, para 49).
	Review of useful life
Usually adjust current and future depreciation by writing the net book value off over the revised remaining useful economic life. However, recognise adjustment to accumulated depreciation as an exceptional item if future results would be materially distorted (para 18).	Adjust depreciation charge for current and future periods (IAS 16, para 52).
	Revaluation
Accumulated deprecation at the date of a revaluation should not be written back to income (para 22).	Case not specifically dealt with, but general rule is that depreciation cannot be so credited (IAS 16, para 35).
	Supplementary depreciation
Depreciation in excess of that based on carrying amount should not be charged to profit and loss (para 16).	(Against spirit of IAS 4.)
	Disclosures
In year of revaluation, the effect of revaluation on the depreciation charge (para 27).	–

3.4 A few issues require brief comment:

Depreciable amount

3.5 The main cause of differences between UK and IASC depreciation here is likely to follow from differences in the rules on revaluation, as examined in Chapter 2.

3.6 Dismantling costs, etc are covered by IAS 16 (see box above), but not addressed by UK rules. Presumably, this need not lead to differences in practice.

Deferral of charge

3.7 IAS 16 (paragraph 43) specifically allows depreciation to be deferred by being debited to the carrying amount of another asset, such as inventory or capitalised development costs. This treatment not addressed by SSAP 12 but would also be UK practice.

Borrowing costs

3.8 The IAS rules on borrowing costs are dealt with by IAS 23 (revised 1993), the main requirements of which are:

- The IAS applies to qualifying assets, which are those which necessarily take a substantial time to get ready for intended use or sale (paragraph 4).

- The benchmark treatment is to expense borrowing costs; the allowed alternative is to capitalise costs that are directly attributable to the acquisition, construction or production of the qualifying asset (paragraphs 7 and 11).

- For funds borrowed specifically, the costs eligible for capitalisation are actual costs less any investment income; for general borrowing, a weighted average of borrowing costs should be used; the amount of borrowing costs capitalised in a period should not exceed the amount of borrowing costs incurred in that period (paragraphs 15 and 17).

- Capitalisation should commence when expenditures, borrowing costs and activities are in progress (paragraph 20).

- Capitalisation should be suspended when active development is interrupted for extended periods and ceased when substantially all the activities are complete for the whole asset or a usable part (paragraphs 23, 25 and 27).

Differences between UK and IASC rules

3.9 Both the UK and the IASC rules allow the capitalisation of interest, but the latter rules are much the more detailed. The following box lists the *differences*.

UK	IASC
Source	
CA 1985, FRS 4	IAS 23
Treatment	
Borrowing costs may be capitalised (Sch 4, para 26).	Benchmark: borrowing costs should be recognised as an expense in the period incurred (para 7). Alternative: borrowing costs may be capitalised when directly attributable to the acquisition, construction or production of an asset (para 10). Other conditions are specified (for example, paras 15, 17 and 23).
Period of capitalisation	
The 'period of production' (Sch 4, para 26).	Commencement of expenditures and borrowing costs are being incurred and activities to prepare the asset for use or sale are in progress (para 20). Suspension should occur during extended interruptions of activity (para 23). Cessation should occur when substantially all the necessary activities are complete (para 25).
Disclosures	
Required to separately disclose amounts transferred from the profit and loss account to the cost of an asset (FRS 4, para 6).	The borrowing cost capitalised in the period (para 29).
The amount of capitalised interest included in the cost of any asset (Sch 4, para 26).	–
–	The capitalisation rate (para 29).

Period of capitalisation

3.10 IAS 23 is much more detailed (see above) than the UK rules on this subject. This seems to mean that compliance with IAS 23 would ensure compliance with UK rules, but that some interpretations of the UK rules would not comply with some of the details of IAS 23.

Taxation

3.11 This topic contains major differences between IASC and UK rules. There is a particular complication in that the new IAS 12 (revised in 1996) does not come into force until accounting periods beginning on or after 1 January 1998. This introduces major differences from UK practice. Until that period, the old IAS 12 (reformatted in 1994) may be used. This allows sufficient options that UK practice can normally be compatible with it. In order to cope with these two regimes, both are examined below.

3.12 Another UK standard is of relevance to accounting for tax. This is SSAP 8 which covers the treatment of tax credits and advance corporation tax. These issues are not covered by IAS 12 but there seem to be no incompatibilities.

IAS 12 before revision

3.13 The differences between the IASC and UK rules currently in force are summarised in the box below.

UK	IASC
Source	
SSAP 8; SSAP 15; FRS 2; FRS 3; CA 1985	IAS 12 (reformatted 1994)
Scope	
Relates primarily to tax on profits and surpluses, but principles should be applied to other taxes (SSAP 15, paras 1 and 2).	Excludes government grants, investment tax credits, split rate systems (para 2).

Deferred tax

Liability method (SSAP 15, para 24).	Deferral or liability method (para 10).
Account for deferred tax to the extent to which it is probable that a liability or an asset will crystallise (SSAP 15, paras 25 and 26).	Normally full provision but can exclude effects of timing differences that are not expected to reverse in three years (para 18).
Debit balances can only be carried forward where they are expected to be recoverable without replacement by equivalent debit balances (SSAP 15, para 30).	Debit balances can only be carried forward if there is a reasonable expectation of realisation (para 19).

Pensions

For deferred tax on pensions and other post-retirement benefits, it is allowed to use either full or partial provision (SSAP 15, para 32A).	–

Profits of subsidiaries

No special rules; account in accordance with SSAP 15 (para 44).	Taxes that would be payable if profits were distributed upwards within the group (or from associates) should be accrued when distribution is probable (paras 34 and 36).

Presentation

Both balance sheet and profit and loss account positions for tax and deferred tax are specified (Sch 4).	–

UK and IASC rules for profit measurement

	Disclosures
Details related to franked investment income, ACT and overseas income (SSAP 8, para 28). Amounts transferred between deferred tax account and profit and loss account (SSAP 8, para 28).	–
Amounts of unprovided deferred tax (SSAP 15, para 35). Rate of tax applied (SSAP 8, para 29). Tax treatment of movement on revaluation reserve (Sch 4, para 34).	–
Extent of provision of deferred tax on future remittances of overseas subsidiaries, or note on lack of provision (SSAP 15, para 44 and FRS 2, para 54).	–
Disclose significant factors affecting current and future tax charge (FRS 3, para 23).	Details of tax losses used or unusable (para 48).

IAS 12 revised

3.14 The revised IAS 12 is very different from its predecessor and from UK rules; it is fairly close to the US standard SFAS 109. The main requirements of the revised IAS 12 are:

- The basis of the calculation of deferred tax is temporary differences between the tax base of an asset or liability and its accounting carrying amount (paragraph 6).

- Deferred tax liabilities should be recognised for taxable temporary differences except those arising from: (i) goodwill (unless tax deductible); (ii) initial recognition of assets or liabilities which do not arise on business combinations and do not affect accounting or taxable profit; and (iii) in some cases, investments in subsidiaries, etc (paragraph 16).

- Deferred tax assets should be recognised for deductible temporary differences except those arising from cases such as (i) to (iii) above (paragraph 24).

- The conditions for exempting temporary differences relating to investments in subsidiaries, etc relate to cases where the investor can control the timing of the reversal of the temporary difference and it is probable that the difference will not reverse in the foreseeable future (paragraphs 39 and 43).

- Deferred tax assets should be recognised for carry forward of tax losses and credits to the extent that it is probable that they can be used (paragraph 34).

- Deferred tax assets and liabilities should be measured using enacted tax rates expected to apply and the expected manner of recovery or settlement of assets and liabilities (paragraphs 46 and 50).

- There should be no discounting (paragraph 52).

- Deferred tax should be recognised as income or expense except for amounts arising on acquisition or transactions taken directly to equity (paragraph 57).

3.15 The main differences between the revised IAS 12 and UK practice are as follows:

UK	IASC
Source	
SSAP 8; SSAP 15; FRS 2; CA 1985	IAS 12 (revised 1996)
Scope	
Relates primarily to tax on profits and surpluses, but principles should be applied to other taxes (SSAP 15, paras 1 and 2).	Excludes government grants, investment tax credits, consequences of dividend payments (paras 4 and 5).
Deferred tax basis	
Accounting for deferred tax on timing differences to the extent that it is probable that an asset or liability will crystallise (SSAP 15, para 25).	Full accounting for deferred tax on temporary differences, with a few exceptions (paras 15 and 23).
Debit balances	
Recognise to the extent expected to be recoverable without replacement by equivalent debit balances (SSAP 15, para 30).	Recognise to the extent that it is probable that taxable profit will be available (paras 23 and 33).

UK and IASC rules for profit measurement

Tax rates

Estimated tax rates; usually the current rate unless changes are known in advance (SSAP 15, para 14).	Expected rates, based on those enacted or substantially enacted (para 45).

Pensions

For deferred tax on pensions and other post-retirement benefits, it is allowed to use either full or partial provision (SSAP 15, para 32A).	–

Profits of subsidiary etc

No special rules; account in accordance with SSAP 15 (para 44).	Recognise deferred tax when it is probable that the temporary differences will reverse in the foreseeable future (para 38). For a deferred tax asset, there is an extra condition that it is probable that taxable profit will be available against which to use the deductible temporary difference (para 43).

Discounting

–	Not allowed (para 52).

Presentation

Both balance sheet and profit and loss account positions for tax and deferred tax are specified (Sch 4).	Tax assets and liabilities should be presented separately from others; and there should be separation of current and deferred tax balances (para 68).

Disclosures

Amounts transferred between deferred tax account and profit and loss account (SSAP 8, para 28).	Numerical reconciliation of difference between effective and applicable tax rates or expense (para 80).
Details related to franked investment income, ACT and overseas income (SSAP 8, para 28).	–
Amounts of unprovided deferred tax (SSAP 15, para 35). Rate of tax applied (SSAP 8, para 29). Tax treatment of movement on revaluation reserve (Sch 4, para 34).	–

43

| Extent of provision of deferred tax on future remittances of overseas subsidiaries, or note on lack of provision (SSAP 15, para 44 and FRS 2, para 54). | Unrecognised amounts in respect of investments in subsidiaries, etc (para 80). |

3.16 In summary, the main practical difference between IAS 12 (revised) and UK practice is that the former demands full allocation while the latter demands partial allocation. However, a further major philosophical difference is that IAS 12 adopts a balance sheet approach, leading to the recognition of deferred tax on temporary differences between the carrying amount and the tax base of an asset or liability. SSAP 15 calculates deferred tax on timing differences between the accounting recognition and the tax recognition of an expense or a revenue. These different philosophies often lead to similar deferred tax results. However, sometimes they do not; for example, the revaluation of an asset generally leads to a temporary difference but not a timing difference.

Extraordinary items etc

3.17 IAS 8 (revised 1993) deals with ordinary and extraordinary items, changes in accounting policy, corrections of fundamental errors and further presentation issues relating to the profit and loss account. The main requirements are:

- Ordinary and extraordinary components should be separately disclosed on the face of the income statement (paragraph 10).

- Ordinary items of abnormal size or incidence must be separately disclosed, usually in the notes (paragraph 16).

- Extraordinary items are clearly distinct from ordinary activities. These are rare, but include expropriation of assets or effects of earthquakes (paragraphs 6 and 14).

- A number of disclosures relating to discontinued operations are necessary (paragraph 20).

- Changes in accounting estimates should be absorbed into income (paragraph 26), but the correction of a fundamental error should be treated as a prior year adjustment (benchmark) or absorbed into income (allowed alternative) (paragraphs 34 and 38).

- A change in accounting policy should be treated in the same way as a fundamental error unless an IAS requires otherwise (paragraph 46).

Differences between UK and IASC rules

3.18 The UK changes in this area which came into force in 1993 as a result of FRS 3 have had major effects on the prevalence of extraordinary items and the presentation of exceptional items. Nevertheless, it may still be possible to interpret IAS 8 in such a way that UK practice is consistent with it. The *differences* between UK and IASC rules are looked at in the following box.

UK	IASC
Source	
FRS 3	IAS 8
Exceptional items	
These result from ordinary activities but have exceptional size or incidence. They include material profits and losses on sale of operations or fixed assets and costs of re-organisation (paras 5 and 20).	Items within ordinary activities which are of such a size, nature or incidence as is relevant to explain performance (para 16). The term 'exceptional' is not used.
Extraordinary items	
Very wide definition of ordinary activities and exceptional items means that there may be no examples of extraordinary items (paras 2, 6 and 20).	Definition refers to activities distinct from ordinary activities, but examples do exist (paras 6, 12-14 and Appendix).

	Presentation
Profits and losses on sales of operations or fixed assets and costs of fundamental re-organisation are shown separately in the profit and loss account after operating profit (para 20). Other exceptional items are included in the appropriate headings in arriving at operating profit, with separate disclosure on the face of the profit and loss account or in the notes (para 19). Extraordinary items (shown net of tax, with tax disclosed separately) would be shown in the profit and loss account before appropriations (para 22).	'Exceptional' items should usually be disclosed in the notes (para 17). Extraordinary items should be shown (net of tax) on the face of the income statement (para 10).
Acquired operations	
Disclosure of acquired operations (as part of continuing operations) on the face of the profit and loss account (para 14).	[See subsidiaries from paragraph 4.2.]
Discontinued operations	
Disclosure of discontinued operations (not as extraordinary) on the face of profit and loss account (para 14).	Details disclosed in notes, although may rarely be an extraordinary item (paras 20 and 21).
Fundamental errors and changes to policies	
Prior period adjustments (para 7).	Benchmark: treat as prior period adjustment (paras 34 and 49). Alternative: include the cumulative adjustment in the current period's income statement (paras 38 and 54).
Disclosures	
–	Nature of fundamental errors and amounts of corrections (para 37).

Revenue recognition

3.19 IAS 18 (revised 1993) contains rules on the above subject. The main elements of IAS 18 are:

- Revenue should be measured at the fair value of consideration received or receivable (paragraph 9).

- Revenue from a sale should be recognised when the seller has transferred control and the significant risks and rewards of ownership; when the consideration and any associated costs can be measured reliably; and when it is probable that economic benefits will flow to the enterprise (paragraph 14).

- When the outcome of a services transaction can be measured reliably, a stage-of-completion basis should be used (paragraph 20). Otherwise revenue should be recognised only to the extent that the expenses are recoverable (paragraph 26).

- Specific criteria are laid down for the recognition of interest, royalty and dividend revenue (paragraph 30).

Differences between UK and IASC rules

3.20 There is no equivalent UK standard to IAS 18, although elements of it are covered in various UK rules and particularly by the CA 1985 rules on realised profits and by FRS 5.

3.21 The following two particular issues covered by IAS 18 could lead to different practice from the UK because there are no UK rules.

Deferred consideration

3.22 IAS 18 considers the appropriate accounting treatment when the receipt of consideration in a cash or cash equivalent form is deferred such that its fair value differs from the nominal amount of the receivable. Discounting at the imputed rate of interest is deemed to be essential where the arrangement constitutes a financing transaction. The Standard goes on to say that the rate is the more clearly determinable of either the prevailing rate for a similar instrument of an issuer with a similar credit rating or a rate that discounts the nominal amount of the receivable to the current cash sales price. The difference would be treated as interest revenue. There is no similar specific requirement on discounting for revenue under UK rules, but it would probably be regarded as necessary in order to give a true and fair view.

Inventory swaps

3.23 IAS 18 also deals with inventory exchanges between suppliers as occurs with oil or milk when inventories in various locations are swapped to fulfil demand on a timely basis in a particular location. IAS 18 makes it clear that this type of exchange is not to be treated as generating revenue. It is not clear whether these swaps should be recognised as turnover in the UK and this would depend on the specific facts.

Pensions

3.24 IAS 19 (revised 1993) deals with retirement benefit costs. Its main requirements are:

- For defined contribution plans, the contributions of a period should be recognised as an expense (paragraph 25).

- For defined benefit plans, the expense in the current period includes:

    - current service cost;

    - current recognition of past service costs, experience adjustments and changes in actuarial assumptions; and

    - results of terminations, settlements or curtailments (paragraph 24).

- Past service costs, experience adjustments and changes in actuarial assumptions relating to existing employees should normally be taken to income over expected remaining working lives (paragraph 28).

- When terminations, curtailment or settlement is probable, cost increases should be charged immediately but any gains should be recognised when the event occurs (paragraph 33).

- For retired employees, plan amendments should be recognised immediately at the present value of the effect of the amended benefits (paragraph 38).

- The benchmark actuarial valuation method is the accrued benefit valuation method, whereas the allowed alternative is the projected benefit valuation method (paragraphs 42 and 44).

- A change in method should be accounted for as a change in accounting policy in accordance with IAS 8 (paragraph 50).

- Actuarial assumptions should include projected salary levels (paragraph 46).

Differences between UK and IASC rules

3.25 The broad approaches of SSAP 24 and IAS 19 are similar. Many of the disclosure requirements also overlap. The following box concentrates on the *differences*. As usual, blanks in one of the columns below mean that there are no specific requirements.

IASC and UK rules for profit measurement

UK	IASC
	Source
SSAP 24	IAS 19
Terminations etc	
When there is a significant reduction in the number of employees covered, related to the sale or termination of an operation, the associated pension cost or credit should be recognised immediately. In all other cases where there is a reduction in contributions due to a significant reduction in employees, the reduction of contributions should be recognised as it occurs. For instance, the effects of a contribution holiday should be spread over its duration (para 81).	When termination, curtailment or settlement is probable, any increase in cost should be recognised immediately. Any gain should be deferred until the event occurs (para 33).
Material deficits	
Where there has been a major event or transaction outside the normal actuarial assumptions which has necessitated significant extra contributions, a material deficit may be recognised over a shorter period than remaining service lives (para 82).	–
Refund subject to tax deduction	
If made in accordance with the Finance Act 1986 etc, a surplus may be accounted for when a refund occurs (para 83).	–
Retired employees	
There are no special rules relating to retired employees, so past service costs should be written off over the remaining service lives of the current employees (para 31).	Effects of plan amendments in respect of retired employees should be measured as the present value of the effect of the amended benefits and should be recognised when the amendment is made (para 38).
Ex gratia pensions or increases	
The capital cost, if not covered by a surplus, should be recognised when granted (paras 84 and 85).	–

–	*Valuation methods* Benchmark: accrued benefit valuation method (para 42). Alternative: projected benefit valuation method (para 44).
Disclosures for defined contribution schemes	
Outstanding or pre-paid contributions (para 87).	–
Disclosures for defined benefit schemes	
Note if actuary is employee or officer (para 88,d). The amount of any deficiency on a current funding level (para 88,g). The percentage level of funding (para 88,h). Commitments to make additional payments for limited period (para 88,i).	–

3.26 Both UK and IASC rules imply the use of long-term discount rates, unlike the US rules in this area. This and the flexibility over valuation methods, suggests that it will often be possible simultaneously to obey UK and IASC rules for pensions. In the cases above where there is no IAS rule (for example, the treatment of ex gratia pensions or unusual deficits), the UK treatment may be acceptable under IAS 19.

3.27 In the UK, UITF 6 extends the principles of SSAP 24 to post-retirement benefits other than pensions. IAS 19 (paragraph 4) states that it is 'appropriate' to apply its rules to such obligations, although there is no requirement to do so.

Chapter 4

IASC and UK rules for group accounting

4.1 This chapter looks at IASC rules and at the differences between them and UK rules in the area of group accounting. Certain related issues are covered in other chapters; for example, segmental reporting is examined in Chapter 5.

Consolidation of subsidiaries

4.2 IAS 27 (reformatted in 1994) deals with consolidated financial statements, although reference to IAS 28 and IAS 31 is needed for associates and joint ventures and to IAS 22 for business combinations.

4.3 The main requirements of IAS 27 are:

- A subsidiary is defined as one controlled by another enterprise (paragraph 6).

- Certain intermediate parent companies are exempted from preparing consolidated accounts (paragraph 8).

- All subsidiaries must be included, except where control is temporary due to expected sale or where there are severe long-term restrictions on the transfer of funds (paragraph 13).

- The reporting dates of consolidated companies should be no more than three months from the parent's (paragraph 19).

Differences between UK and IASC rules

4.4 The *differences* between UK and IASC rules are summarised in the box and some are examined in more detail below.

UK	IASC
Source	
FRS 2; CA 1985	IAS 27
Definitions	
An additional definition of subsidiary is where there is a participating interest and either actual exercise of dominant influence or the existence of unified management (FRS 2, para 14(e)).	–
Exemption from preparation of consolidated accounts	
Small or medium groups and wholly-owned non-listed subsidiaries of parents in the EU. Less than wholly-owned subsidiaries with parents in the EU, under certain conditions (FRS 2, para 21).	Wholly-owned or (with approval of minorities) virtually wholly-owned subsidiaries (para 8).
Accounting periods	
Unless impractical, interim financial statements should be prepared when year ends differ (FRS 2, para 43).	–
Presentation	
Minority interests have defined positions in profit and loss accounts and balance sheets (Sch 4).	Minority interests must be shown in a balance sheet separately from liabilities and parent shareholders' equity (para 26).
Dissimilar subsidiaries	
Exclusion on grounds of dissimilarity is required in exceptional circumstances, but is expected to be rare (FRS 2, para 25). The equity method should then be used (FRS 2, para 30).	No exclusion (para 11).
Disposals	
The calculation of gain or loss on sale should include the goodwill not amortised through the profit and loss (FRS 2, paras 45-47).	–

UK and IASC rules for group accounting

Disclosures	
Nature and extent of restrictions on access to distributable profit (FRS 2, para 53).	[See Cash flow statements from paragraph 5.2.]
Extent of provision of deferred tax on future remittances of overseas subsidiaries, or note on lack of provision (FRS 2, para 54).	[See Taxation, topic 3.11.]
Details on cessation of subsidiaries (FRS 2, paras 48 and 49).	–
Details of subsidiaries with different year ends from the parent (FRS 2, para 44).	–
Details on excluded subsidiaries (FRS 2, para 31).	–
[See Extraordinary items, topic 3.4.]	Effect of acquired and disposed subsidiaries on the results (para 32).

Definition of subsidiary

4.5 IAS 27's definition of a subsidiary rests on control, which is the power to govern the financial and operating policies. The UK rules in FRS 2, FRS 5 and the Companies Act are much more complex, but would generally lead to the same conclusion. However, the UK rules generally require a parent to be an investor in an enterprise for it to be a subsidiary. This seems not to be the case under IAS 27.

Exemptions

4.6 The UK rules allow a parent enterprise that is itself a subsidiary to be exempted under various conditions. However, IAS 27 only allows this when the enterprise is wholly owned or virtually wholly-owned, with a 90 per cent threshold suggested.

Presentation

4.7 The UK practice of showing minority interests as an item between shareholders' funds and liabilities is acceptable under IAS 27, although it also allows minorities to be shown as part of total shareholders' funds, but not part of parent shareholders' funds. Both FRS 4 and IAS 32 would

55

require elements of minority interests to be treated as liabilities, if they meet the definition of a liability.

Dissimilar subsidiaries

4.8   The difference between the UK and IAS rules as above is, in practice, usually unimportant. Although, the UK rules seem to require exclusion in certain cases, the Companies Act states that this does not mean merely dissimilarity because some subsidiaries are industrial, some commercial, etc. FRS 2 (paragraphs 25 and 78) suggests that these cases are very exceptional.

Disposals

4.9   Unlike FRS 2, there are no requirements in IAS 27 on the subject of whether the calculation of gain or loss on disposal of a subsidiary should include any goodwill initially written off to reserves. Although IAS 22 (revised) requires goodwill to be capitalised and amortised, this only came into force in 1995, without the need for retrospective application. This means that, if a group chooses not to bring any written off goodwill into its calculation of gain on disposal, the gain may be much larger than under UK rules.

Associates

4.10   IAS 28 (reformatted in 1994) deals with the treatment of associates in group accounts and in investor accounts. The latter issue is covered in Section 2.3 in this book. As far as group accounting is concerned, IAS 28 requires the following:

- An associate is an enterprise over which the investor has significant influence, that is, the power to participate in financial and operating policy decisions (paragraph 3). This is a rebuttable presumption when there is a holding of 20 per cent or more in the voting rights (paragraph 4).

- Associates should be accounted for by the equity method in consolidated accounts, unless held for disposal in the near future (paragraph 8).

Differences between UK and IASC rules

4.11 The *differences* between IASC and UK rules are listed in the box below.

UK	IASC
Source	
SSAP 1; CA 1985	IAS 28
Treatment if no consolidated accounts	
Prepare additional financial statements or add supplement to existing statements (SSAP 1, paras 24 and 35).	Option to use equity method or cost method with a note of what the equity method would have shown (IAS 28, para 14).
Profit shares using equity method	
Show profit before tax (SSAP 1, para 19).	No instruction.
Disclosures	
Loans to and from associates; share of reserves; restrictions on distribution; shareholdings in associates (SSAP 1, paras 27, 28, 31, 40, 49).	–

4.12 As may be seen by the small number of items in the box above, IAS 28 is largely consistent with UK rules. One connected issue is that IAS 28 allows the use of the equity method in the investor's individual accounts, but that is dealt with in Section 2.3 on investments.

4.13 Neither IAS 28 nor UK rules deal with the issue of the elimination of gains and losses on transactions between the investor and the associate, but a proportional elimination seems appropriate.

Joint ventures

4.14 IAS 31 (reformatted in 1994) deals with accounting for joint ventures in group accounts. The treatment in the individual accounts of a venturer is discussed in Section 2.3 of this book. The main requirements of IAS 31 are:

- A joint venture involves a contractual agreement leading to joint control (paragraph 2).

- Joint ventures can be divided into three jointly controlled types: operations, assets and entities (paragraph 3).

- Venturers should account for the part of the operations that they control (paragraph 10).

- Venturers should proportionally account for assets (paragraph 16).

- Venturers may choose between proportional consolidation and equity accounting for entities (paragraphs 25 and 32).

- However, entities under severe long-term restrictions or acquired and held for re-sale should be treated as investments (paragraph 35).

- Gains and losses on transactions between the venturer and the venture should generally be eliminated (paragraphs 39 and 40).

Differences between UK and IASC rules

4.15 The differences between IAS 31 and UK rules are summarised in the following box and commented on after that.

UK	IASC
Source	
SSAP 1; CA 1985	IAS 31
Types of venture	
Distinction between unincorporated and incorporated ventures (SSAP 1, para 18; Sch 4A, paras 19 and 20).	Distinction between jointly controlled operations, assets and entities (para 3).
Incorporated entities	
Use equity method (Sch 4A, para 20).	Benchmark: proportional consolidation (para 25). Allowed alternative: equity method (para 32).
Assets	
By implication proportional consolidation or the equity method are allowed (Sch 4A, para 19).	Proportional consolidation (para 16).

4.16 IAS 31 is much more detailed than the UK rules on the subject of how and when to use proportional consolidation. However, it would seem generally possible to choose options in the two sets of rules to enable conformity with both.

4.17 For jointly controlled operations, where there is no joint venture entity, IAS 31 requires the venturer to account for its own assets, etc. Presumably, this would be the result under UK rules.

4.18 For jointly controlled assets, the UK rules are not specific, so presumably it would be possible to follow IAS 31's requirement of proportional consolidation.

4.19 For jointly controlled unincorporated entities, both sets of rules allow a choice of proportional consolidation and the equity method.

4.20 For jointly controlled incorporated entities, IAS 31 allows a choice, which includes the UK requirement for the equity method.

Acquisitions and mergers

4.21 IAS 22 (revised 1993) contains requirements relating to business combinations. Its main requirements are:

- A uniting of interests is a combination where an acquirer cannot be identified (paragraph 9). This is an exceptional case (paragraph 14). Indications of an acquisition are:

    - when the fair value of one enterprise is significantly greater than that of the other;

    - when cash is used to buy voting shares;

    - when the management of one enterprise dominates the selection of managers of the combined enterprise;

    - when financial arrangements provide a relative advantage to one group of shareholders; or

    - when one party's share of the equity in the combined enterprise depends on the performance of its former part of the business.

- Unitings of interest must be accounted for by the pooling of interest method, but all other combinations must be accounted for as purchases (paragraphs 18 and 61).

Differences between UK and IASC rules

4.22 The rules of FRS 6 and IAS 22 are very similar. Both require the use of merger accounting (pooling) for a very restricted class of business combinations. Some significant differences are noted in the following box and discussed below.

UK	IASC
Source	
FRS 6	IAS 22
Terminology	
Merger	Uniting of interests
Merger accounting	Pooling of interests
Acquisition	Acquisition
Acquisition accounting.	Purchase accounting.
Criteria for merger accounting	
Restriction to those cases allowed by company law (para 5).	–
Reverse acquisitions	
Legal parent is the acquirer (Appendix II).	Enterprise whose shareholders now control the combined enterprise is the acquirer (para 13).

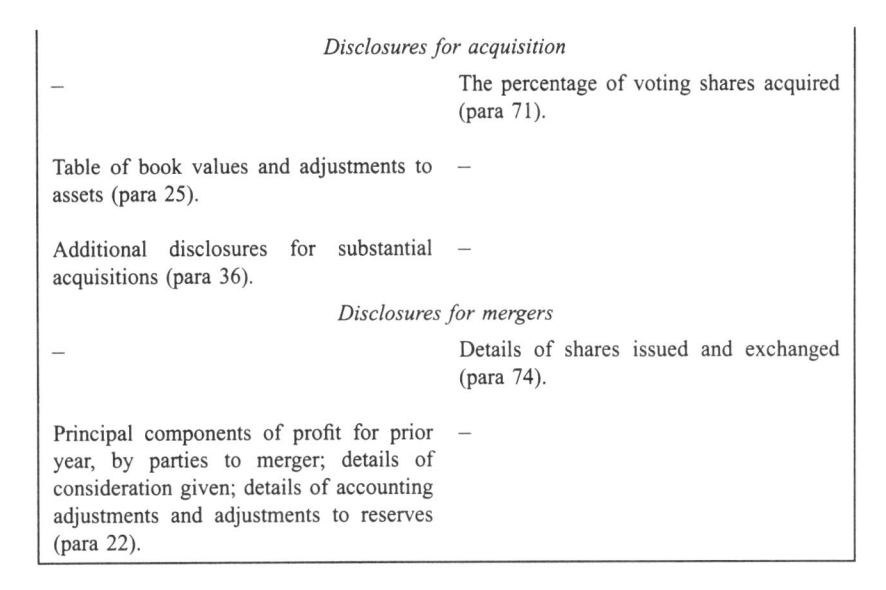

	Disclosures for acquisition
–	The percentage of voting shares acquired (para 71).
Table of book values and adjustments to assets (para 25).	–
Additional disclosures for substantial acquisitions (para 36).	–
	Disclosures for mergers
–	Details of shares issued and exchanged (para 74).
Principal components of profit for prior year, by parties to merger; details of consideration given; details of accounting adjustments and adjustments to reserves (para 22).	–

Criteria for merger accounting

4.23 Both FRS 6 and IAS 22 have some detailed criteria for determining whether there is merger/uniting of interests. However, FRS 6 explains its criteria in more detail. For example, IAS 22's 'significantly greater' (paragraph 12) comparison of the combining parties is specified in FRS 6 (paragraph 68) as one party being more than 50 per cent larger than the other.

4.24 The legal restriction on the use of merger accounting in the UK is unlikely to be a problem in practice because FRS 6 applies more stringent criteria than the Companies Act does.

Reverse acquisitions

4.25 IAS 22 takes a 'substance over form' approach to identifying the acquirer in the case of a reverse acquisition. FRS 6 notes that IAS 22's rule would seem to be illegal in the UK. This suggests that the legal parent should be treated as the acquirer, However, it may be possible to override this by reference to the 'true and fair view' in particular cases.

Goodwill and fair values

4.26 IAS 22 (revised 1993) contains the requirements on goodwill and fair values. The main instructions are:

- For an acquisition, individual assets and liabilities should be recognised if it is probable that an economic benefit will flow and if there is a reliable measure of cost or fair value to the acquirer (paragraph 27).

- Assets and liabilities of the acquired company are brought into the consolidated financial statements at fair value. The difference between the cost of the purchase and the fair value of the net assets is recognised as goodwill. The benchmark treatment is not to apply fair valuation to the minority's proportion of net assets; the allowed alternative is to fair value the whole of the net assets (paragraph 31 and 33).

- Fair values are calculated by reference to intended use by acquirer (paragraph 28).

- Goodwill must be capitalised and amortised over five years, or longer (up to twenty years) if this can be justified (paragraphs 40 and 42).

- The benchmark treatment for negative goodwill is to reduce the non-monetary assets proportionately and to treat any balance as deferred income (paragraph 49).

- The allowed alternative is to treat negative goodwill as deferred income (paragraph 51).

4.27 In 1996, the IASC decided to review IAS 22 with respect to relaxing the maximum limit of 20 years for the amortisation of goodwill and changing the rules for negative goodwill.

Differences between UK and IASC rules

4.28 The revised (1993) version of IAS 22 introduced several important differences from UK practice. Nevertheless, by appropriate choice of UK and IASC options it would sometimes be possible to prepare financial statements that were largely compatible with both sets of rules. This book concentrates on the *differences* in the rules.

UK	IASC
Source	
SSAP 22; FRS 7; UITF 3	IAS 22
Positive goodwill	
Option of immediate write off to reserves or amortisation over useful life (SSAP 22, paras 39 and 41).	Goodwill must be treated as an asset and amortised over five years or, if justified, up to twenty years (para 42). Any amounts not supported by future benefits should be expensed (para 46).
Negative goodwill	
Credit to reserves (SSAP 22, para 40).	Benchmark: reduce the values of non-monetary assets. Any excess is deferred income (para 49). Alternative: treat negative goodwill as deferred income. Amounts should be amortised over five years or, if justified, up to twenty years (para 51).
Fair values	
Use arm's length market prices reflecting conditions at the date of acquisition (FRS 7, paras 2 and 6).	Use of acquirer's perspective (para 38).
Minority interests	
Shown at proportion of fair values (SSAP 22, para 36).	Benchmark: show them at the proportion of pre-acquisition book values (para 31). Alternative: a complete fair value exercise (para 33).

Subsequent recognition	
Provisional recognition and measurement should be adjusted in the financial statements for the first full financial year following the acquisition, with a corresponding adjustment to goodwill (FRS 7, para 24). Any adjustment after that, except for correction of fundamental errors, should go to income (FRS 7, para 25).	If assets and liabilities meet criteria at some point after acquisition, they should then be recognised. Similarly, carrying amounts of assets or liabilities should be adjusted when additional evidence becomes available. This may lead to an adjustment of goodwill, provided that this is recoverable and is made by the end of the first annual accounting period commencing after acquisition. Otherwise, adjustments go to income (para 58).
Sale of business	
Profit on sale should take account of previously written off goodwill (UITF 3).	–

Positive goodwill

4.29 IAS 22's requirement relating to capitalisation and amortisation of goodwill is one of the major areas of difference between UK practice and IAS rules. It would be possible for a UK company to follow the IAS, but this is unusual in practice. However, there are proposals to amend SSAP 22 (see FRED 12 of 1996) and forthcoming proposals to amend IAS 22. This may bring practice closer.

Fair values

4.30 IAS 22's requirement to use an acquirer's perspective when measuring fair value means that valuations take account of the acquirer's intentions for the future. This may include, for example, provisions for reorganisations or for impairment of assets resulting from events after acquisition. Such things cannot be taken into account under FRS 7. Therefore IAS 22's net asset values are likely to be lower (and goodwill higher) than under FRS 7.

Minority interests

4.31 IAS 22's benchmark for fair valuation in the context of minority interests is not consistent with SSAP 22, but the allowed alternative is.

Sale of business

4.32 Since IAS 22 does not require retrospective compliance, many companies complying with it may have written off goodwill to reserves in the past. When they come to sell the related subsidiaries, there is no instruction about the treatment of such goodwill. By contrast, UITF 3 requires it to be taken into account in the calculation of profit on sale of the subsidiary. Consequently, such profit under IAS 22 might be much larger than under UK rules.

Currency translation of financial statements

4.33 IAS 21 (revised 1993) includes rules on the translation of the financial statements of foreign operations or entities. Its main requirements are:

- The financial statements of foreign operations that are 'integral' to the operations of the parent should be treated as if the transactions had been those of the reporting enterprise (paragraph 27).

- Financial statements of other entities should be translated using closing rates for balance sheets and transaction rates (or, in practice, average rates) for income and expenses. Exchange differences should be taken to reserves (paragraph 30).

- The financial statements of a foreign entity in a hyperinflationary economy should be restated according to IAS 29 before translation (paragraph 36).

- On disposal, the cumulative amount of deferred exchange differences in reserves should be taken to income (paragraph 37).

4.34 Translation of foreign currency monetary items in individual accounts is also dealt with by IAS 21, but is covered by Topic 2.6 in this book.

Differences between UK and IASC rules

4.35 There is broad agreement between SSAP 20 and IAS 21. For example, closing rates are generally to be used for balance sheet items and resulting differences should generally be taken to reserves. Also, disclosure requirements are largely similar. However, there are some differences in optional treatments and some issues are dealt with in more detail by one or other of the documents (hence the blanks in the following box).

UK	IASC
\multicolumn{2}{c}{Scope}	
SSAP 20; UITF 9	IAS 21
\multicolumn{2}{c}{Profit and loss items}	
Closing rate or average rate (SSAP 20, para 54).	Actual (or average) rate (paras 30 and 31).
\multicolumn{2}{c}{Hyperinflation}	
Two treatments are allowed for translation of operations in hyperinflationary economies (UITF 9): (a) adjusting their financial statements to their local price levels before translation; or (b) using a stable currency as functional (that is, using the temporal method with respect to that currency).	Foreign financial statements should be restated in accordance with IAS 29 (for example, using price indices to adjust historical cost fixed assets) (para 36).
–	In this case the closing rate should be used for income and expense items (para 30).
–	Where the economy ceases to be hyperinflationary and IAS 29 is no longer used, the entity should use the amounts expressed in the measuring unit at the date of discontinuation as the historical costs (para 36).
\multicolumn{2}{c}{Disposal}	
–	On disposal of a foreign entity, the deferred cumulative exchange differences should be recognised in income (para 37).
\multicolumn{2}{c}{Disclosure}	
–	Details of changes in classification between net investment (entities) and closely-held (integral operations) (para 44).

Integral operations

4.36 Both IAS 21 and SSAP 20 require integral operations to be translated as if all the transactions had been entered into by the reporting enterprise. SSAP 20 refers to the use of the temporal method, but this amounts to the same thing.

4.37 The classification of foreign operations into integral and other depends, in both standards, on the use of rather vague criteria, which seem to be broadly consistent. In practice, this may allow companies to chose whether or not to use the closing rate method.

Hyperinflation

4.38 IAS 29's proposed treatment seems to be consistent with method (a) of UITF 9.

Disposal

4.39 IAS 21 contains the instruction to take the cumulative deferred exchange differences into the calculation of the gain or loss on disposal of foreign operations. There is no such instruction in UK rules and it is not normally done, which leads to a difference in practice.

Chapter 5

IASC and UK rules in other areas

5.1 This chapter deals with IASC rules and with differences between them and UK rules in several areas of presentation and disclosure which have not been examined in detail in previous chapters.

Policies, disclosures, formats

5.2 IASs 1, 5 and 13 (all reformatted in 1994) contain rules under this heading. They will all be replaced by a standard based on E 53, 'Presentation of Financial Statements', (which was issued in 1996). The main present requirements are:

- Fundamental assumptions are going concern, consistency and accrual. If they are not followed, that should be disclosed (IAS 1, paragraph 3).

- Prudence, substance over form and materiality should govern selection and application of policies (IAS 1, paragraph 5).

- All significant accounting policies should be disclosed (IAS 1, paragraph 8).

- Inappropriate accounting is not rectified by disclosure (IAS 1, paragraph 16).

- The name of the reporting enterprise, its country of incorporation, the balance sheet date and the period of account should be disclosed (IAS 5, paragraph 7).

- Corresponding figures for the previous year should be shown (IAS 5, paragraph 9).

- A large list of minimum disclosures is given (IAS 5).

- It is not necessary to classify assets and liabilities into current and non-current (IAS 13, paragraph 7).

- Partial definitions of current assets and current liabilities are given (IAS 13).

- The current portion of a long-term liability can be excluded from current liabilities if there is an intention and reasonable reassurance of ability, to refinance the obligation on a long-term basis (IAS 13, paragraph 16).

- Set-offs between current assets and current liabilities should not be made unless there is a legal right of set-off and an expectation of using it (IAS 13, paragraph 20).

Differences between UK and IASC rules

5.3 In this very broad area, there are many similarities between UK and IASC rules. Some important differences are noted in the following box.

UK	IASC
Source	
SSAP 2; FRS 4; FRS 5; CA 1985	IAS 1; IAS 5; IAS 13
Prudence	
Regarded as overriding (SSAP 2, para 14). Fundamental but not specified as overriding (Sch 4, para 12).	Not regarded as fundamental (IAS 1, para 5).
Substance over form	
Required when not directly covered by other instructions (FRS 5, para 14).	Required when selecting accounting policies and preparing financial statements (IAS 1, para 7).
Formats	
Standard formats (with some choice) are specified for the balance sheet and profit and loss account (Sch 4).	–
Current assets and liabilities	
Current assets and liabilities must be presented separately from non-current items (Sch 4). Current assets are those not intended for continuing use in the business (s 262(1)). Current liabilities are those falling due within one year (Sch 4).	There is no generic definition of 'current', nor any instruction to present current items separately from non-current (IAS 13).

Current portion of long-term liabilities	
May be treated as non-current where there are committed facilities for refinancing (FRS 4, para 35).	May be treated as non-current where there is intention and ability to refinance (IAS 13, para 16).
Set-off	
There should be determinable monetary amounts and no doubt about ability to insist on net settlement (FRS 5, para 29).	Legal right and expectation of using it (IAS 13, para 20).

Prudence

5.4 In the UK, the attitude to prudence has gradually changed. SSAP 2 was issued in 1971, when prudence was accepted as overriding. After the development of the conceptual framework in the US, prudence was downgraded, as is reflected in the IASC's conceptual framework and in IAS 1. The British Companies Act (originally the 1981 Act) also does not treat prudence as overriding; and UK standard setters have often made decisions which seem to treat prudence in a somewhat cavalier fashion (for example, taking gains on unsettled long-term currency items in SSAP 20). However, for preparers and auditors, prudence will still be an important background concept when interpreting either UK or IASC rules.

Formats

5.5 At present, there are no general instructions on formats under IASC rules, unlike the position for the UK. However, the IASC issued proposals for presentation in E 53 in 1996. This stops short of mandatory formats but would require certain items to be disclosed on the face of financial statements.

Cash flow statements

5.6 IAS 7 (revised 1992) contains the requirements on cash flow accounting. The main ones are that:

- Cash flow statements are required (paragraph 1).

- They should classify cash flows into operating, investing and financing activities (paragraph 10).

- Cash and cash equivalents include short-term investments subject to insignificant risk of changes in value (paragraph 6).

- Either the direct or indirect method is allowed (paragraph 18).

- Cash flows should be reported gross, with a few exceptions (paragraphs 21 to 24).

- Cash flows from transactions in a foreign currency or those of a foreign subsidiary should be translated at the date of the cash flows (paragraphs 25 and 26).

- Cash flows associated with extraordinary items should be classified under one of the three headings and disclosed (paragraph 29).

- Cash flows from taxes should be disclosed separately within one of the three headings (paragraph 35).

- Aggregate cash flows from acquisitions and disposals of subsidiaries or other units should be presented separately under investing activities (paragraph 39).

- Transactions not involving the use of cash or cash equivalents should be excluded from the cash flow statement but disclosed elsewhere (paragraph 43).

- There should be disclosure and reconciliation with the balance sheet of components of cash and cash equivalents (paragraph 45).

- There should be disclosure of significant balances not available for use by the group (paragraph 48).

Differences between UK and IASC rules

5.7   On the whole, FRS 1 and IAS 7 are similar. However, there are some important differences, examined below.

IASC and UK rules in other areas

UK	IASC
	Source
FRS 1	IAS 7
	Scope
Exemptions for small enterprises, wholly-owned subsidiaries, building societies and mutual life assurance companies (para 8).	–
	Definitions
Cash equivalents must be without notice and within three months of maturity when acquired. Cash equivalents are calculated after deduction of advances from banks repayable within three months (para 3).	No such strict limitations as in FRS 1 (para 6), but guidance based on three months (para 7).
	Format
Five sections are to be used: operating; returns on investment and servicing of finance; taxation; investing activities; financing (para 12).	Three sections are to be used: operating; investing; financing (para 10). Interest, dividends and taxes should be shown under the appropriate heading, usually 'operating' (paras 31 and 33).
	Net or gross
The cash flow statement should include all inflows and outflows of cash and cash equivalents except for purchases and sales of cash and cash equivalents, that is, they should be shown gross (para 11).	Cash flows from investing and financing should be shown gross, except under certain conditions (para 21).
	Foreign currencies
Use exchange rate as in profit and loss account (para 36).	Use exchange rate at date of cash flow (paras 25 and 26).
	Disclosures
[See Subsidiaries, topic 4.1.]	Amount of cash and equivalents not available for use (para 48).
Reconciliation of movements in the financing section with the balance sheet (para 44).	–

5.8 In 1995, the UK's ASB issued an exposure draft (FRED 10) which would move UK rules further away from IAS 7. At the time of writing, this is due for release soon.

Contingencies and post balance sheet events

5.9 IAS 10 (reformatted in 1994) contains the requirements in this area, including:

- Contingent losses should be accrued if probable and capable of estimation (paragraph 8).

- Disclosure should be made of other contingent losses, unless remote (paragraph 9).

- There should not be provision for general or unspecified risks (paragraph 15).

- Virtually certain gains can be accrued (paragraph 17); probable contingent gains are disclosed (paragraph 16).

- Events occurring after the balance sheet date which provide additional information on conditions existing at that date should lead to adjustment of the financial statements (paragraph 25).

- However, disclosure should be made for other events, if unusual (paragraph 28).

Differences between UK and IASC rules

5.10 UK and IASC rules on contingencies and on post balance sheet events are very similar. Some small differences are noted below.

UK	IASC
Source	
SSAP 8; SSAP 17; SSAP 18	IAS 10
Dividends	
Proposed and declared dividends should be accrued (SSAP 8, para 26).	Proposed or declared dividends should be accrued or disclosed (para 31).

IASC and UK rules in other areas

	Disclosures
The estimate of the financial effect of a contingency should exclude tax effects, which should be separately noted (SSAP 18, para 20).	–
The reversal or maturity of a transaction designed to alter the balance sheet (SSAP 17, para 23).	–

Dividends

5.11 The UK treatment as noted in the above box is implied by SSAP 8. Since there is no such requirement under IAS 10, IAS practice might omit a debit to reserves and a credit to current liabilities for such proposed or declared dividends.

Segmental reporting

5.12 IAS 14 (reformatted in 1994) contains the rules on segmental reporting. The main requirements are:

- Unusually for an IAS, the standard restricts its coverage to 'publicly traded or other economically significant entities' (paragraph 2).

- There should be industry and geographical segment disclosures of:

    - sales;
    - result;
    - assets employed;
    - the basis of inter-segment pricing (paragraph 16).

- There should be a reconciliation between the sum of the individual segments and aggregate information (paragraph 21).

5.13 At the time of writing, proposals to produce a revision of IAS 14 are at an advanced stage.

Differences between UK and IASC rules

5.14 Broadly, SSAP 25 and IAS 14 have similar requirements. However, the former is more detailed and leads to greater disclosures. The *differences* are examined in the following box.

UK	IASC
Source	
SSAP 25; CA 1985	IAS 14
Scope	
Companies Act applies to all companies but contains only requirements relating to turnover (Sch 4, para 55). SSAP 25 applies only to (i) PLCs or entities with PLCs as subsidiaries, (ii) banks or insurance companies, (iii) large companies (ten times Companies Act criteria) (SSAP 25, para 40).	Publicly traded companies and other economically significant entities (para 2).
Exemption	
Exemption where disclosure would be seriously prejudicial (SSAP 25, para 43).	–
Segments	
Threshold of 10 per cent of turnover, result or net assets is normal (SSAP 25, para 9).	–
Turnover by origin, but also by destination if materially different (SSAP 25, para 34).	Turnover by origin implied (para 16).
Net assets are normally non-interest bearing assets less non-interest bearing liabilities (SSAP 25, para 34).	Disclosure of segmented liabilities is not normal (para 19).
Associates	
Aggregate of shares of associates' pre-tax results and net assets (where this is 20 per cent or more of total) (SSAP 25, para 36).	–
Disclosure	
–	Basis of inter-segment pricing (para 16).

Segments

5.15 Both IAS 14 and SSAP 25 have lengthy discussions on how one might use judgement in determining reportable segments.

5.16 IAS 14 does not have a numerical threshold of significance for reportable segments, although it does refer (paragraph 15) to the possibility of using 10 per cent.

Changing prices

UK

5.17 There are some disclosure requirements relating to inventories, investments and land, which involve the provision of information when current values are materially different from book values (CA 1985, Sch 4, paras 27 and 45; and Sch 7, para 1).

IASC

5.18 IAS 15 would require certain disclosures concerning adjustments to reflect changing prices. Enterprises should disclose the following information on a general purchasing power or a current cost basis:

- depreciation adjustment;
- cost of sales adjustment;
- monetary items adjustment; and
- the overall effect of the above and any other adjustments.

5.19 However, in 1989 the IASC decided that it was not necessary to comply with the standard in order to conform with IASs.

5.20 IAS 29 relates particularly to enterprises or groups reporting in the currency of a hyperinflationary economy (indicated by such factors as a cumulative rate of inflation in three years of 100 per cent; paragraph 3). The major requirements can be summarised as:

- Financial statements and prior year figures should be shown in units current at the balance sheet date (paragraph 38).

- The gain or loss on the net monetary position should be included in income and separately disclosed (paragraph 39).

- There should be disclosure of methods used (paragraph 41).

5.21 It should be noted that IAS 29 relates to primary financial statements not merely to notes. Also, it is not merely designed as part of the exercise of including hyperinflationary foreign subsidiaries in group accounts, although it is relevant for that process (see topic 4.6).

Related party disclosures

5.22 IAS 24 (reformatted in 1994) contains the instructions in this area, including that:

- Related parties are those able to control or exercise significant influence, though some exceptions are noted (paragraphs 5 and 6).

- Control relationships should be disclosed (paragraph 20).

- Related party transactions should be disclosed (paragraph 22).

- Items of a similar nature may generally be disclosed in aggregate (paragraph 24).

- Exemptions relate to (paragraph 4):

    - Intra-group transactions in group accounts.
    - Parent accounts that are published with group accounts.
    - Wholly-owned subsidiary's accounts under certain circumstances.
    - Transactions between state-controlled enterprises.

Differences between UK and IASC rules

5.23 FRS 8 and IAS 24 contain very similar requirements. The important differences are noted in the following box:

UK	IASC
	Source
FRS 8	IAS 24
	Related parties for part of year
If parties are related at any time in the financial period, they are treated as related for the whole period (para 2).	Issue not dealt with.
	Exemptions
Group transactions in accounts of 90 per cent or more owned subsidiaries, provided group accounts are publicly available (para 3).	Accounts of wholly-owned subsidiaries, with a parent in the same country providing consolidated accounts (para 4).
	Disclosures
Names of transacting related parties; amounts due to or from related parties; amounts written off such debts in the period (para 6).	–

Exemptions

5.24 The exemptions relating to subsidiaries are noticeably different between IAS 24 and FRS 8. The former does not require any disclosures in the accounts of wholly-owned subsidiaries. The latter's exemption relates to 90 per cent or more owned subsidiaries but only exempts transactions with entities that are part of the group or related party investees.

Chapter 6

IASC's work in progress

6.1 As noted in Chapter 1, IASC has stepped up its work programme, towards completion of a set of core standards designed to satisfy IOSCO. Consequently, many major additions and changes to IASC rules can be expected in the last few years of the 1990s. Of course, major changes to UK rules are also anticipated; some of them as a result of, or in co-ordination with, IASC changes.

6.2 IASC projects in progress include:

- *Segmental reporting.* IASC proposes to revise and expand its segmental reporting requirements. The likely direction of change can be gauged from E 51 of 1996. This proposes that an enterprise should usually report primary segments on the basis of management's organisation of the business, which might be a line-of-business or a geographical segment basis. Less detailed disclosures would be required for secondary segments. The UK's ASB published a discussion paper on this in 1996, with a view to minimising the differences between a revised IAS and the UK rules.

- *Earnings per share.* E 52 of 1996 proposes to require EPS disclosures from enterprises with publicly traded securities. The 'earnings' figure would be the net profit. The 'per share' calculations would be required on both basic and diluted bases. The UK's ASB published a discussion paper on this issue in 1996, with a view to minimising differences between the eventual IAS and the UK rules.

- *Intangible assets.* E 50 of 1995 proposed that identifiable intangible assets should be recognised when it is probable that future economic benefits will flow to the enterprise and when the cost of the asset can be measured reliably. The benchmark valuation basis would be amortised cost, but an allowed alternative would be revaluation by class of assets, to fair value. The allowed alternative only applies in cases where there is an active secondary market. The general amortisation requirements impose a limit of the shorter of twenty

81

years and useful life. However, in 1996 exceptions were proposed for certain cases and these are still being debated. This latter issue has led to a review of IAS 22's goodwill rules.

- *Presentation of financial statements.* E 53 of 1996 deals with the compulsory contents of financial statements, including notes. It would replace IASs 1, 5 and 13. An important feature is the introduction of a 'statement of non-owner movements in equity', which is somewhat similar to the UK's statement of total recognised gains and losses. Fair presentation would be required for the financial statements, although not to the extent of overriding any requirement of an IAS. As in IAS 13, a current non-current split is not required. A list of minimum headings for the face of the financial statements is given, but no standardised formats are set out. There is also a list of minimum disclosures for the notes. Enterprises would have to disclose that they are complying with IASs and should qualify statements of compliance for any departures.

- *Interim reporting.* The IASC produced a draft statement of principles on interim reporting in 1996. This adopts the view that interim periods should generally be treated as discrete periods, so that there should not be smoothing across a whole year. It seems likely that IASC and future UK requirements can be brought into line.

- *Discontinuing operations.* The IASC produced a draft statement of principles on discontinuing operations in 1996. It is presently proposed that discontinuing operations should be separately disclosed from the date of irrevocable commitment. This would be somewhat different from the UK position in FRS 3, whereby separate reporting is required for operations which have already discontinued. Furthermore, the IASC proposes to define 'operations' in a similar way to 'segments', whereas FRS 3 includes material reductions in scale.

- *Financial instruments.* IAS 32 already deals with some presentation and disclosure issues relating to financial instruments. However, measurement issues (which were included in E 40 and E 48) are still being discussed. It is too early to predict the conclusions with confidence.

- *Other projects.* There are several other topics at an early stage of consideration:

    - agriculture.
    - impairment of assets.
    - provisioning.
    - revision of IAS 17 (leases).
    - revision of IAS 19 (pensions).

Chapter 7

Summary and concluding remarks

7.1 This book has examined IASC's financial reporting rules and the material differences between them and UK rules. There are many smaller differences of wording which may lead to differences of interpretation or to differences in the details of disclosures.

Compatibility of UK and IASC rules until 1993

7.2 Up until the end of 1993, there had been few important inconsistencies between UK and IASC rules. In some areas, UK rules were more detailed or covered topics not covered by the IASC. There were also examples of the opposite of this. In some cases there were options in UK or IASC rules which allowed any particular company to obey both sets of rules. The net result was that most UK standards could say *"Compliance with the requirements of this Statement will automatically ensure compliance with International Accounting Standard X"*. In some cases, the words *"in all material respects"* were included, without explanation.

7.3 In the IASC's *Survey of Use and Application of International Accounting Standards* (concluded in 1993, but not published), the UK is shown as a country where rules and practice coincide closely with IASs. Table 7.1 is compiled from several tables in that draft publication.

Compatibility after 1993

7.4 In earlier chapters, it has been noted that several major changes to IASs were agreed at the end of 1993 and were effective from 1995.

Compatibility of UK rules or practices with IASs

7.5 These changes led to several significant cases where UK requirements or normal UK practice is inconsistent with IASs. Major examples of this are listed in Tables 7.2 and 7.3.

Summary and concluding remarks

7.6 There are also some cases where UK rules or practice are not consistent with an IAS's benchmark treatment but are consistent with an allowed alternative. These are listed in Table 7.4. In these particular cases, there is no requirement in the IAS for reconciliations to the benchmark. However, this latter issue may become relevant if overseas securities' regulators specify IASs (or particular treatments in them) for cross-border filings.

Table 7.1 – Compliance of UK rules with IASs

IAS		UK Score
1	Disclosure	3
2	Inventories	3
4	Depreciation	3
5	Disclosures	3
7	Cash flow	3
8	Extraordinary items etc	3
9	R&D	3
10	Contingencies	3
11	Construction contracts	3
12	Taxes	3
13	Current assets	3
14	Segments	3
15	Changing prices	6
16	Property, plant	3
17	Leases	3
18	Revenue recognition	4
19	Retirement costs	3
20	Government grants	3
21	Foreign exchange	3
22	Business combinations	3
23	Borrowing costs	4
24	Related parties	6
25	Investments	3
26	Retirement plans	3
27	Consolidation	3
28	Associates	3
30	Disclosure by banks	4
31	Joint ventures	3

Source: access to an IASC draft publication (see text) is gratefully acknowledged.

Scores in Table 7.1 on page 86
1 =   IAS adopted as a national requirement.
2 =   IAS used as the basis for a national requirement.
3 =   National requirement developed separately and conforms in all material respects with IAS.
4 =   No national requirements but national practice generally conforms with IAS.
5 =   National requirement developed separately but does not conform with IAS.
6 =   No national requirements and national practice does not generally conform with IAS.

Table 7.2 – Some inconsistencies between UK rules and IASs

IAS 7 *Cash flow statements.* The IAS has three standard headings, whereas FRS 1 has five.

IAS 8 *Extraordinary items.* The IAS's definition, though similar to that of FRS 3, does at least have some items in this category.

IAS 12 *Deferred tax.* The revised IAS requires full accounting for deferred tax on temporary differences, whereas SSAP 15 requires partial accounting on timing differences.

IAS 22 *Fair values.* The IAS requires the use of the acquirer's perspective whereas FRS 7 requires a neutral/market perspective.

IAS 22 *Goodwill.* For negative goodwill, the IAS has a benchmark treatment (write down non-monetary assets) and an allowed alternative treatment (defer and amortise). However, neither of these is the same as the UK practice of crediting negative goodwill to reserves.

IAS 32 *Financial instruments.* The IAS requires instruments to be classified on the basis of their substance and that compound instruments should be split into parts on that basis. However, the UK rules rest more on legal form, which does not involve splitting.

Table 7.3 – Cases where common UK practice is inconsistent with IASC rules (although IASC rules could be obeyed)

IAS 9 *Development expenditure.* The IAS requires development expenditure which meets certain criteria to be capitalised. Such capitalisation is allowed by SSAP 13, but is only minority practice in the UK.

IAS 16 *Property, plant and equipment.* The IAS's benchmark is historical cost. The allowed alternative is regular revaluation by class of asset. However, many UK companies have carried out irregular valuations of selected assets.

IAS 21 *Currency translation.* The IAS requires the use of the average rate for profit and loss account items. Many UK companies choose to use the closing rate.

IAS 22 *Goodwill.* The IAS requires the capitalisation of goodwill and its amortisation over up to five years (or possibly up to 20). This treatment is possible under the UK's SSAP 22, assuming that the useful economic life can be interpreted as the number of years specified by IAS 22. However, nearly all UK companies choose SSAP 22's preferred option of immediately writing goodwill off against reserves.

Table 7.4 – Cases where UK rules or practice are inconsistent with an IASC benchmark but consistent with an allowed alternative

IAS 22 *Goodwill.* The IAS's benchmark treatment when there is a minority interest is to calculate fair values in relation only to the group's share of net assets. UK requirements (FRS 2) are that a full fair value exercise should be carried out, though not attributing any goodwill to the minority. This UK treatment is the IAS's allowed alternative.

IAS 31 *Joint ventures.* The IAS's benchmark treatment is proportional consolidation. For incorporated joint ventures, the UK rules require equity accounting, which is the IAS's allowed alternative.

7.7 Table 7.5 summarises the degree of compatibility between UK rules and IASs (as issued by the end of 1996). In the 'rules' column, a '✓' suggests compatibility of material issues. The cases with an '×' are those incompatibilities noted in Table 7.2. Although there are also inconsistencies in the rules on extraordinary items, UK practice may usually be acceptable under IASs. In the 'options' column of Table 7.5, there are further cases (shown by an '×') where important UK options are not compatible with IAS rules. These are the cases of Table 7.3.

Compatibility of IASs with UK rules

7.8 Looking from the opposite direction, there are also cases where IAS rules or options are not acceptable in the UK. The cases where IAS *rules* are unacceptable are those covered in Table 7.2. The cases where IAS *options* are unacceptable are shown in Table 7.6. Table 7.7 summarises the acceptability of IAS rules and practice in the UK.

Implications of the incompatibilities

7.9 These newly arrived incompatibilities between IAS and UK rules or practices have created difficulties in the UK. Of course, the 'compliance with IAS' paragraphs in UK standards will have to be reconsidered. However, the main point is that it has become much more inconvenient for UK companies to comply with IASs, although few of them had anyway been making positive statements about compliance. A further implication may be that the Accounting Standards Board will be encouraged to review UK standards in order to reduce the differences from IASs. There is evidence of this already happening, as noted under several of the headings in Chapter 6. Presumably, pressure to reduce the differences will get stronger if IOSCO accepts IASs for cross-border listings and particularly if the SEC accepts them for reporting by UK companies listed on the New York Stock Exchange. In the longer run, it will be necessary to face the question of whether we need UK standards as well as IASs.

Table 7.5 – Compatibility of UK rules with IASs (published by 1996)

IAS*		UK rules acceptable under IAS	UK options unacceptable under IAS
1	Disclosure	✓	–
2	Inventories	✓	–
4	Depreciation	✓	–
5	Disclosures	✓	–
7	Cash flow	×	–
8	Extraordinary items etc	×	–
9	R&D	✓	×
10	Contingencies	✓	–
11	Construction contracts	✓	–
12	Taxes	×	–

Summary and concluding remarks

13	Current assets	✓	–
14	Segments	✓	–
16	Property, plant	✓	×
17	Leases	✓	–
18	Revenue recognition	✓	–
19	Retirement costs	✓	–
20	Government grants	✓	–
21	Foreign exchange	✓	×
22	Business combinations:		
	mergers	✓	–
	fair values	×	–
	goodwill	✓	×
	negative goodwill	×	–
23	Borrowing costs	✓	–
24	Related parties	✓	–
25	Investments	✓	–
27	Consolidation	✓	–
28	Associates	✓	–
31	Joint ventures	✓	–
32	Financial instruments	×	–

*Certain IASs have been omitted here; see Appendix II

Table 7.6 – Cases where IAS optional practice is inconsistent with UK rules

IAS 2   *Inventories.* The IAS allowed alternative of LIFO is not normally acceptable in the UK.

IAS 8   *Exceptional items, discontinued operations, newly acquired operations.* The UK rules in FRS 3 require many disclosures on the face of the income statement which are not required by the IAS.

IAS 8   *Prior period items.* The IAS's allowed alternative treatment for the correction of fundamental errors or for changes in accounting policies is to include them in current income. This is not acceptable under FRS 3.

IAS 13 *Current assets and liabilities.* The option not to classify assets and liabilities is not acceptable in the UK for most companies.

IAS 20 *Government grants.* The option to deduct a grant from the carrying value of an asset is not acceptable for most companies in the UK.

IAS 25 *Investment.* The optional treatment of investment properties under IAS 25 is not consistent with the requirement of SSAP 19.

IAS 31 *Joint ventures.* The benchmark treatment of proportional consolidation is not acceptable for incorporated joint ventures in the UK.

Summary and concluding remarks

Table 7.7 – Compatibility of IASs with UK rules

IAS*		IAS rules acceptable in UK	IAS options unacceptable under UK rules
1	Disclosure	✓	–
2	Inventories	✓	×
4	Depreciation	✓	–
5	Disclosures	✓	–
7	Cash flow	×	–
8	Extraordinary items etc	×	×
9	R&D	✓	–
10	Contingencies	✓	–
11	Construction contracts	✓	–
12	Taxes	×	–
13	Current assets	✓	×
14	Segments	✓	–
16	Property, plant	✓	–
17	Leases	✓	–
18	Revenue recognition	✓	–
19	Retirement costs	✓	–
20	Government grants	✓	×
21	Foreign exchange	✓	–
22	Business combinations:		
	mergers	✓	–
	fair values	×	–
	goodwill	✓	–
	negative goodwill	×	–
23	Borrowing costs	✓	–
24	Related parties	✓	–
25	Investments	✓	×
27	Consolidation	✓	–
28	Associates	✓	–
31	Joint ventures	✓	×
32	Financial instruments	×	–

*Certain IASs have been omitted here; see Appendix II

Appendix 1

UK and IASC rules

Extant UK statements of standard accounting practice

Explanatory foreword (revised August 1986)
SSAP 1   Accounting for associated companies (revised April 1982 and by ASB interim statement in 1990)
SSAP 2   Disclosure of accounting policies
SSAP 3   Earnings per share (amended October 1992)
SSAP 4   Accounting for government grants (revised July 1990 and amended October 1992)
SSAP 5   Accounting for value added tax
SSAP 8   The treatment of taxation under the imputation system in the accounts of companies (revised December 1977 and amended October 1992)
SSAP 9   Stocks and long-term contracts (revised September 1988)
SSAP 12 Accounting for depreciation (revised January 1987 and amended October 1992)
SSAP 13 Accounting for research and development (revised January 1989)
SSAP 15 Accounting for deferred tax (revised May 1985 and December 1992)
SSAP 17 Accounting for post balance sheet events
SSAP 18 Accounting for contingencies
SSAP 19 Accounting for investment properties (amended October 1992 and July 1994)
SSAP 20 Foreign currency translation
SSAP 21 Accounting for leases and hire purchase contracts
SSAP 22 Accounting for goodwill (revised July 1989 and amended September 1994)
SSAP 24 Accounting for pension costs (amended October 1992)
SSAP 25 Segmental reporting

Appendix 1

Financial reporting standards

Foreword to accounting standards
FRS 1   Cash flow statements
FRS 2   Accounting for subsidiary undertakings
FRS 3   Reporting financial performance (amended June 1993)
FRS 4   Capital instruments
FRS 5   Reporting the substance of transactions (amended December 1994)
FRS 6   Acquisition and mergers
FRS 7   Fair values in acquisition accounting
FRS 8   Related party disclosures

UITF pronouncements

Foreword to UITF abstracts
1   Convertible bonds – supplemental interest/premium (withdrawn by FRS 4)
2   Restructuring costs (withdrawn by FRS 3)
3   Treatment of goodwill on disposal of a business
4   Presentation of long-term debtors in current assets
5   Transfers from current assets to fixed assets
6   Accounting for post-retirement benefits other than pensions
7   True and fair view override disclosures
8   Repurchase of own debt (withdrawn by FRS 4)
9   Accounting for operations in hyperinflationary economics
10   Disclosure of directors' share options
11   Capital instruments: issuer call options
12   Lessee accounting for reverse premiums and similar incentives
13   Accounting for ESOP trusts
14   Disclosure of changes in accounting policy
15   Disclosure of substantial acquisitions

Appendix 1

Extant IASC standards

Preface (revised 1983)
Objectives and procedures (including the constitution; revised 1982)
Framework for the preparation and presentation of financial statements (1989)

IAS 1	Disclosure of accounting policies
IAS 2	Inventories
IAS 4	Depreciation accounting
IAS 5	Information to be disclosed in financial statements
IAS 7	Cash flow statements
IAS 8	Net profit or loss for the period, fundamental errors and changes in accounting policies
IAS 9	Research and development costs
IAS 10	Contingencies and events occurring after the balance sheet date
IAS 11	Construction contracts
IAS 12	Accounting for taxes on income
IAS 13	Presentation of current assets and current liabilities
IAS 14	Reporting financial information by segment
IAS 15	Information reflecting the effects of changing prices
IAS 16	Property, plant and equipment
IAS 17	Accounting for leases
IAS 18	Revenue
IAS 19	Retirement benefit costs
IAS 20	Accounting for government grants and disclosure of government assistance
IAS 21	The effects of changes in foreign exchange rates
IAS 22	Business combinations
IAS 23	Borrowing costs
IAS 24	Related party disclosures
IAS 25	Accounting for investments
IAS 26	Accounting and reporting by retirement benefit plans
IAS 27	Consolidated financial statements and accounting for investments in subsidiaries
IAS 28	Accounting for investments in associates
IAS 29	Financial reporting in hyperinflationary economies
IAS 30	Disclosure in the financial statements of banks and similar 'financial institutions'
IAS 31	Financial reporting of interests in joint ventures
IAS 32	Financial instruments: disclosure and presentation

Appendix 2

Equivalence between UK and IASC rules

UK standards and IAS equivalents

UK standard	Title (abbreviated)	IAS equivalent
SSAP 1	Associated companies	28, 31
SSAP 2	Disclosure of accounting policies	1, 5, 13
SSAP 3	Earnings per share	–
SSAP 4	Government grants	20
SSAP 5	Value added tax	–
SSAP 8	Taxation under the imputation system	12
SSAP 9	Stocks and long-term contracts	2, 11
SSAP 12	Depreciation	4, 16
SSAP 13	Research and development	9
SSAP 15	Deferred tax	12
SSAP 17	Post balance sheet events	10
SSAP 18	Contingencies	10
SSAP 19	Investment properties	25
SSAP 20	Foreign currency translation	21
SSAP 21	Leases	17
SSAP 22	Goodwill	22
SSAP 24	Pension costs	19
SSAP 25	Segmental reporting	14
FRS 1	Cash flow statements	7
FRS 2	Subsidiaries	27
FRS 3	Financial performance	8
FRS 4	Capital instruments	32
FRS 5	Substance of transactions	32
FRS 6	Acquisition and mergers	22
FRS 7	Fair values	22
FRS 8	Related party transactions	24

UK SSAPs omitted from the list above and Appendix 1

SSAP 6	Extraordinary items and prior year adjustments (replaced by FRS 3)	
SSAP 7	Current purchasing power accounting (withdrawn)	

Appendix 2

SSAP 10 Statements of source and application of funds (replaced by FRS 1)
SSAP 11 Deferred tax (replaced by SSAP 15)
SSAP 14 Group accounts (replaced by FRS 2)
SSAP 16 Current cost accounting (withdrawn)
SSAP 23 Accounting for acquisitions and mergers (replaced by FRS 6)

IASs and UK equivalents

IAS	Title (abbreviated)	UK equivalent
1	Disclosure of accounting policies	SSAP 2; CA 1985
2	Inventories	SSAP 9; CA 1985
4	Depreciation	SSAP 12; CA 1985
5	Information to be disclosed	CA 1985
7	Cash flow statements	FRS 1
8	Extraordinary items etc	FRS 3
9	Research and development	SSAP 13; CA 1985
10	Contingencies and post balance sheet events	SSAPs 17&18
11	Construction contracts	SSAP 9
12	Taxes on income	SSAPs 8&15; CA 1985
13	Current assets and liabilities	CA 1985
14	Segmental reporting	SSAP 25
16	Property, plant and equipment	CA 1985
17	Leases	SSAP 21; UITF 12
18	Revenue recognition	–
19	Retirement benefits	SSAP 24; UITF 6
20	Government grants	SSAP 4
21	Foreign exchange	SSAP 20; UITF 9
22	Business combinations	SSAP 22; UITF 3; FRS 6&7
23	Capitalisation of borrowing costs	CA 1985
24	Related party disclosures	FRS 8
25	Investments	SSAP 19; CA 1985; UITF 4
27	Consolidated financial statements	FRS 2; CA 1985
28	Investments in associates	SSAP 1; CA 1985
29	Hyperinflationary economies	–
31	Joint ventures	SSAP 1; CA 1985
32	Financial instruments	FRSs 4&5; UITF 11

Appendix 2

Standards omitted from the above list

3 Consolidated financial statements (replaced by IAS 27)
6 Responses to changing prices (replaced by IAS 15)
15 Reflecting effects of changing price (non-mandatory from 1989)
26 Reporting by retirement benefit plans
30 Disclosures by banks etc

Coopers & Lybrand

Coopers & Lybrand UK offices

London – City office
Plumtree Court
London EC4A 4HT
Tel: (0171) 583 5000
Fax: (0171) 822 4652

London – Central office
1 Embankment Place
Villers Street
London WC2N 6NN
Tel: (0171) 583 5000
Fax: (0171) 822 4652

London – West
Harman House
1 George Street
Uxbridge UB8 1QQ
Tel: (01895) 273333
Fax: (01895) 256413

London – South
Melrose House
42 Dingwall Road
Croydon CR0 2NE
Tel: (0181) 681 5252
Fax: (0181) 760 0897

Aberdeen
32 Albyn Place
Aberdeen AB1 1YL
Tel: (01224) 210100
Fax: (01244) 576183

Armagh
3-5 Market Street
Armagh BT61 7BW
Tel: (01861) 522695
Fax: (01861) 526820

Bangor
Railway Court
Bangor BT20 3BU
Tel: (01247) 497968
Fax: (01247) 270603

Belfast
Fanum House
108 Great Victoria Street
Belfast BT2 7AX
Tel: (01232) 245454
Fax: (01232) 242416

Birmingham
Temple Court
35 Bull Court
Birmingham B4 6JT
Tel: (0121) 265 5000
Fax: (0121) 265 5050

Bournemouth
Hill House
Richmond Hill
Bournemouth BH2 6HR
Tel: (01202) 294621
Fax: (01202) 556978

Bristol
Bull Wharf
Redcliff Street
Tel: (0117) 929 2791
Fax: (0117) 929 0810

Cambridge
Abacus House
Castle Park
Gloucester Street
Cambridge CB3 0AN
Tel: (01223) 460055
Fax: (01233) 64036

Cardiff
Churchill House
Churchill Way
Cardiff CF1 4XQ
Tel: (01222) 237000
Fax: (01222) 223361

Derby
Wilmot House
St. James's Court
Friar Gate
Derby DE1 1BT
Tel: (01332) 372936
Fax: (01332) 254080

Dungannon
16 Northland Row
Dungannon
Co. Tyrone BT71 6AP
Tel: (01868) 722726
Fax: (01868) 727324

Edinburgh
Erskine House
68-73 Queen Street
Edinburgh EH2 4NH
Tel: (0131) 226 4488
Fax: (0131) 260 4008

Glasgow
Kintyre House
209 West George Street
Glasgow G2 2LW
Tel: (0141) 248 4444
Fax: (0141) 221 8256

Gloucester
Lennox House
Beaufort Buildings
Spa Road
Gloucester GL1 1XD
Tel: (01452) 423031
Fax: (01452) 300699

Leeds
Albion Court
5 Albion Place
Leeds LS1 6JP
Tel: (0113) 243 1343
Fax: (0113) 231 4590

Leicester
Charnwood Court
New Walk
Leicester LE1 6TG
Tel: (0116) 285 3000
Fax: (0116) 285 3200

Liverpool
Richmond house
1 Rumford Place
Liverpool L3 9QS
Tel: (0151) 227 4242
Fax: (0151) 227 4575

Maidstone
Orchard House
10 Albion Place
Maidstone ME14 5DZ
Tel: (01622) 672961
Fax: (01622) 758071

Manchester
Abacus Court
6 Minshull Street
Manchester M1 3ED
Tel: (0161) 236 9191
Fax: (0161) 247 4000

Milton Keynes
Central Business Exchange
Midsummer Boulevard
Central Milton Keynes
MK9 2DF
Tel: (01908) 690064
Fax: (01908) 690065

Newcastle upon Tyne
Hadrian House
Higham Place
Newcastle upon Tyne
NE1 8BP
Tel: (0191) 261 2121
Fax: (0191) 232 6534

Northampton
Oriel House
55 Sheep Street
Northampton NN1 2NF
Tel: (01604) 230770
Fax: (01604) 238001

Norwich
The Atrium
St George's Street
Norwich NR3 1AG
Tel: (01603) 615244
Fax: (01603) 631060

Nottingham
Cumberland House
35 Park Row
Nottingham NG1 6FY
Tel: (0115) 950 3500
Fax: (0115) 947 0862

Omagh
43 Market Street
Omagh BT78 1EE
Tel: (01662) 246100
Fax: (01662) 246283

Plymouth
Midland House
Notte Street
Plymouth PL1 2EJ
Tel: (01752) 267441
Fax: (01752) 673514

Portadown
43 High Street
Portadown BT62 1HY
Tel: (01762) 333718
Fax: (01762) 350201

Reading
9 Greyfriars Road
Reading RG1 1JG
Tel: (01734) 597111
Fax: (01734) 607700

Sheffield
1 East Parade
Sheffield S1 2ET
Tel: (0114) 272 9141
Fax: (0114) 275 2573

Southampton
5 Town Quay
Southampton SO14 2HJ
Tel: (01703) 632772
Fax: (01703) 330493

Swansea
Princess House
Princess Way
Swansea SA1 5LH
Tel: (01792) 473691
Fax: (01792) 476857

Coopers & Lybrand is a member of Coopers & Lybrand International, a limited liability association incorporated in Switzerland.
Copyright ©1996 Coopers & Lybrand (United Kingdom firm). All rights reserved. Designed by Coopers & Lybrand Design Services. Printed in the United Kingdom.
The UK member firm is authorised by the Institute of Chartered Accountants in England and Wales to carry on investment business.